SUMMER FOOD IN PROVENCE

Other titles by the same author:

Novels:
Entertaining Angels
Childish Things
Breathing Space
Travelling Light
There is a Season
Just Dessert, Dear
Time Out

Essays:
Where the Heart Is
Short Circuits

Children's and youth books:
Rhinocephants on the Roof
Mia's Mom
The Hidden Life of Hanna Why

First edition in 2010 by Tafelberg,
an imprint of NB Publishers,
40 Heerengracht, Cape Town 8001

Printed and bound by Tien Wah Press (Pte) Ltd, Singapore

ISBN 978-0-624-04721-6

SUMMER FOOD IN PROVENCE

MARITA VAN DER VYVER

in association with Alain Claisse

Tafelberg

CONTENTS

BIENVENUE – WELCOME

"TO EAT IS A NECESSITY, BUT TO EAT INTELLIGENTLY IS AN ART."
FRANÇOIS DE LA ROCHEFOUCAULD (1613-1680)

You don't have to live in France to learn to eat well. Everywhere in the world there are noted cooks and food writers who speak no French or understand only a few key phrases such as bouillon, bouquet garni and pot-au-feu. But if you do live in France, it is impossible not to learn to eat better.

Everything that you see, hear, smell, feel and taste sharpens your senses for greater gastronomic enjoyment. It's an experience that begins before birth and continues throughout life. Even the glass jars and plastic tubs of baby food sold here are more interesting than in other countries. Instead of the usual insipid carrot purée or apple mush, French *bébés* are treated to artichokes, courgettes and ratatouille.

From kindergarten French children are provided with a four-course meal in the school restaurant, served in sequence, never all lumped together. Yesterday my nine-year-old daughter's school menu began with *endive au bleu* (chicory with crumbled blue cheese), followed by thick rib of lamb with white beans, then *bûche de chèvre* (a kind of goat's milk cheese), with strawberry sponge roll for dessert.

Grandparents in old age homes also dine better than in other countries. The grandfather of all French gastronomes, Jean Anthelme Brillat-Savarin, speculated that *gourmandise* is often the last earthly pleasure that remains when we grow old – to compensate for all the others we have lost.

No wonder, then, that so many of the most famous food writers and cooks of the past century owed their culinary awakening to a sojourn in France: Elizabeth David, MFK Fisher, Julia Child, to name but a few. Julia Child was already in her thirties when her husband's work brought them to France. *"I was 32 when I started cooking,"* she writes; *"up until then, I just ate."*

I know far less about food than these great names, but my passion was also ignited only when I came to live in France. I fell in love with a Frenchman – and at the same time with the food that he prepared for me with such obvious pleasure (truly a case of finding the way to a woman's heart through her stomach). With Alain, preparing food became real fun for the first time in my life. We enjoy ourselves hugely in the kitchen. Alain peels onions and sings as he weeps, I stir soup and listen to rock music; we talk, taste, tease and sniff at fruit, vegetables and herbs. In short, we cook, literally and figuratively.

Let me make it quite clear however that he is the chef and I the *sous-chef*. In the kitchen, if not elsewhere, I know my place. I often make the first courses, the salads, the desserts, but the main course is Alain's domain. He not only has more experience and confidence at the stove than I do; he also has enough chemical knowledge to understand why such and such happens in an oven or pan when you do this or that. All those mysterious processes, such as sauces that bind or thicken or reduce, which seem to me like sorcery, are science to him.

And yet he cooks more with his heart than his head. It's almost impossible for him to make a dish in exactly the same way twice. Where is the excitement if you know exactly how the end product is going to taste, look and smell even before you begin? Ingredients and herbs vary according to the season and what is available on the market stalls and our kitchen windowsill. *Au pif,* the French call this casual style of cooking. Measures are often vague – a cup, a pinch, or that wonderful French word, a *soupçon,* a suspicion. This is how Alain's mother cooked, and how most French recipes are passed on from mother to daughter (or son), and this is also how we cook in our kitchen.

As far as we are concerned, this is how every self-respecting cook should go to work. Recipes are guidelines, not religious tracts. Naturally there are exceptions such as cakes and other baking where precise quantities are crucial and that's probably why I am the baker in our house. I am more modest, less obstreperous, when it comes to taking direction. Or maybe I'm simply not French enough. No ancestors of mine ever chopped off a king's head. Perhaps it's just that I submit more easily to a higher authority.

Because I remember very well how it feels to be a novice in the kitchen – enthusiastic, adventurous, but at the same time anxious and uncertain – I have tried my best to give precise instructions for all the recipes in this book, with suggestions for substitute ingredients, ideas for similar dishes and explanations of less well known cooking terms. The purpose throughout is to inspire the less experienced cook without boring the more experienced one – and to encourage all cooks to experiment, even if it sometimes leads to failure. As Clifton Fadiman puts it in his preface to MFK Fisher's unsurpassed *The Art of Eating*: "*She never loses sight of the fact that we struggle to gastronomy's altitudes only through the foothills of pots and pans and kitchen stoves and meats and vegetables and many tastings and humiliating failures.*"

The next time you take one of those humiliating failures out of the oven, please remember Samuel Beckett's winged words, "*No matter. Try again. Fail again. Fail better.*" Not only a lesson in the art of cooking, but also a precious lesson in life. And before you rush off to the kitchen to try again, a last word about what I suppose I must describe as our food philosophy – although philosophy sounds very grand for an approach that boils down to a combination of imagination, common sense and a love of good food with practical considerations.

We are an average family with average children (who will not hesitate to choose bought hamburgers and *frites* over all their parents' "gastronomic altitudes") and an average income. We do not have the time, energy or money to make complicated and pretentious dishes with expensive ingredients such as truffles or *foie gras* and our children have no interest in snails, frogs' legs and other French specialities that are hard to obtain elsewhere anyway. The recipes in this book are for the food that we enjoy every summer under the plane tree in our front garden – dishes of Provençal, Mediterranean or general French origin that may just as easily be enjoyed under a jacaranda or a kiepersol in South Africa.

To sum up: we try to eat as well and as sensibly as possible for as little money, time and trouble as possible. We use fresh seasonal produce, preferably from our own garden, town or region, which today makes ecological as well as economic sense. Too much plastic is used for packaging, too much fuel wasted, too many toxins released by unnecessary food miles when you eat a bowl of fresh strawberries in the middle of winter. It may seem smart, but it's actually stupid. There's a time for everything – and late spring and early summer is strawberry time in our part of the world. Then we eat our fill before they disappear from the market stalls until next spring.

When the scarlet strawberries become scarce, splendid melons begin to appear in their place. They are followed by an endlessly surprising variety of beans. Then come the downy apricots and, when summer is almost over, the honey-sweet late figs. After that it's time for the first wild mushrooms of autumn. But that's another story. This book is about spring food, summer food, outdoor food. Food enjoyed with our children, with guests and friends in the shade of our plane tree. *Bon appétit.*

INSPIRING ASPARAGUS

"ASPARAGUS SEEMS TO INSPIRE GENTLE THOUGHT."

CHARLES LAMB (1775-1834)

If asparagus does indeed inspire benign thoughts, it's a real shame that two centuries ago these lissom members of the lily family were so expensive that only aristocratic diners could afford them. Otherwise the French king Louis the Sixteenth, who adored asparagus, might not have lost his head. Quantities were cultivated all year round for his pleasure; if only he had shared a few with his bloodthirsty subjects they might not have dragged him to the guillotine. Imagine, even the formidable Robespierre thinking gentle thoughts over a dish of tender green asparagus.

Thank heaven that asparagus is no longer beyond the purse of the low-born gastronome. In our house, however, it remains a rare pleasure, because in rural France the asparagus season is gone in the twinkling of an eye. Scarcely a month passes from the joyful day when we espy the first bunches on the market tables to the despairing one when there is not a single spear to be had anywhere. And so for us spring always begins with this very important ritual. We eat the first asparagus of the year – and we eat it outside under our plane tree, at the round table which has spent the whole winter in the darkness of the attic.

When the purple irises begin blooming along the roadsides and the plane tree starts slowly unfurling its leafy umbrella over our heads, we know it's time to carry the table outside. We scrub it clean, cover it with a large Provençal cloth patterned with sunflowers or olives and begin to dine alfresco. We continue to eat outside, midday and evenings, twice a day, as long as the weather allows. Right until the end of spring, when the yellow broom and the red poppies splash the landscape with exuberant colour. Right through the summer, when the cicadas serenade us at lunch time like a Mexican mariachi band. Right into autumn, when the heavy bunches of grapes in the vineyards are harvested and the very air around us smells like wine.

Only in late autumn, when the plane's now enormous leaves turn brown and the sun becomes too feeble for outdoor dining even at lunch time, do we carry the table back to the attic, heavily, like a coffin. Until next spring, when once again we head outdoors to feast on the first asparagus.

We prefer the thin green ones to the fat white ones; predictably, because we live in the heartland of the renowned green asparagus of Vaucluse. According to the great chef Auguste Escoffier, all asparagus in Provence were once white – until he personally persuaded a group of farmers to grow the green ones instead. (The difference is that white asparagus grow under the soil like roots, while the green ones grow above the ground and are thus exposed to sunlight.)

Many people remain nervous of cooking any kind of asparagus because it can be tricky to get the stems tender without the tips being reduced to mush. The secret is simply to snap off the hardest part of the stem; unlike the leaves of a chequebook, the asparagus tears naturally at the right place. Shave off the skin of the lower stem with a potato peeler and then you can lay the whole spear flat in a pot, like a baby in a bed.

The greatest treason you can commit against the noble asparagus is to cook it too long. Then you might just as well go and buy its limp cousin in a can.

The Emperor Augustus, another long-ago lover of asparagus, even thought up a saying for anything that had to be done quickly: *Velocius quam asparagi coquantur.* "Faster than you can cook asparagus."

However you decide to cook your asparagus, remember that a few drops of lemon juice and a shaving or two of Parmesan is always preferable to drowning the lovely lily in a pool of bought mayonnaise.

ASPARAGI COQUANTUR . . .
If your asparagus are really fresh, you don't need to boil them. Grill them, for a taste experience in a class of its own. Spread the spears in a shallow pan or on a baking sheet, brush both sides with olive oil and place under a hot grill for 5-10 minutes, turning them regularly. When golden brown flecks begin to appear, they are ready. Serve on a bed of rocket, corn salad and other baby leaves, garnished with spring onion and paper-thin slices of radish and drizzled with a classic French vinaigrette. (See Indispensable on page 177.)

Or bake the asparagus, brushed with olive oil for 5-10 minutes in a preheated oven at 200 °C, together with a few sprigs of rosemary, half a lemon and slices of *jambon cru* or smoked ham. Take the dish out of the oven, squeeze over the juice of the hot lemon, drizzle with more olive oil, season with a few turns of the pepper mill and serve on a *mesclun* salad (mixed young salad leaves). Or bake them on their own, squeeze over the juice of half a lemon and garnish with torn coriander leaves.

ASPARAGUS IN A BLANKET
(GRATIN D'ASPERGES)
SERVES 4

24 green asparagus spears | 300 ml pouring cream | 200 ml chicken stock | freshly grated nutmeg | 4 slices cooked ham | 15 g butter | 125 g grated cheese | salt and pepper

In a largeish pot, boil enough salted water to just cover the asparagus. Add the spears and cook for about 10 minutes until tender but still firm. Drain carefully.

In a smaller pot, simmer the cream and chicken stock until reduced by half. Add nutmeg, salt and pepper to taste and remove from the heat.

Divide the asparagus into four portions. Roll each bunch tightly in a slice of ham and place in an oven-proof dish greased with the butter. Pour over the cream mixture, scatter with grated cheese and bake in a preheated oven at 200 °C for 20-25 minutes, or until the cream blanket takes on a golden colour. Serve at once.

STRIPED ASPARAGUS
SERVES 4

12 green asparagus spears | 12 white asparagus spears | 4 T olive oil | 1 T French Banyuls vinegar (or Italian balsamic vinegar) | a handful of chopped chervil (can be replaced with parsley or coriander; see Indispensable on page 177) | 100 g Parmesan cheese | salt and pepper

Snap off the tough ends of the asparagus and peel with a potato peeler. Steam for about 10 minutes and drain.

Mix the olive oil, vinegar, chervil, salt and pepper to make a salad dressing.

Halve the warm asparagus lengthwise, arrange on a large platter (or on a bed of assorted salad leaves), drizzle with the dressing and garnish with shavings of Parmesan. Serve while still lukewarm.

Right: Asparagus in a blanket

ORIENT AND IMMORTAL WHEAT

"ORIENT AND IMMORTAL WHEAT . . . I THOUGHT IT HAD
STOOD FROM EVERLASTING TO EVERLASTING."

THOMAS TRAHERNE (CIRCA 1637-1674)

Did you think couscous was an Arabian dish? So did I, until I found out that the French had "nationalised" it long ago. Which is more or less what our South African forefathers did with bobotie, koeksisters and other good things originally brought by the slaves from the East to the refreshment station at the Cape.

This lesson I learnt almost thirty years ago, when I came to work in southwest France as an au pair for a young couple. Their brown-eyed baby was to be my charge and I realised very quickly that while my university degree in French might perhaps have equipped me to write an essay on Camus or Sartre, it was absolutely no help when it came to discussing baby bottles, nappy rash and other matters of vital importance. The parents could not speak any English and the baby was too young to speak anything at all. After our first week of faltering communication, they invited me to a "typical French meal" with friends, presumably hoping to find a guest who could act as interpreter between us.

I remember a long table with a patterned cloth and a huge window overlooking the sea. I remember cool white wine poured from earthenware jugs. And I remember the Police singing very loudly over the sound system – the British pop group was very big in France that summer. Not far from where I found myself, my future husband attended one of their concerts, but it would be nearly twenty years before we got to know each other. What I remember most clearly, though, is the food. In my ignorance I had assumed that "typically French" meant something like *coq au vin* or a Burgundian stew. Instead I was completely surprised by a magnificent *couscous royal*.

A pile of steaming grains, fiery merguez sausages and other types of meat, colourful vegetables in bright earthenware bowls and a fragrant, reddish sauce with a spicy kick … my first couscous. Although the word originally referred only to the grain that forms the foundation of the dish, in France is has become the name of this entire, royal feast.

This was the first of many I was to taste down the years, because couscous is the French equivalent of curry and rice – food for church bazaars, school fetes and other such occasions. When French people gather around a few tables in a town hall to raise funds for anything from a political party to a new boules court, ten to one they'll be given *couscous royal* to eat. Because it consists of a wide selection of vegetables and at least three kinds of meat, served in separate dishes, there's something for every taste, vegetarian or carnivore. The fiery sauce – which is not for timid diners – is also served separately.

Couscous is derived from the lovely Arabic name *kuskus* (which always makes me think of an Afrikaans kiss) and is actually coarse-ground semolina that is rolled in a specific kind of flour while damp. Our Moroccan neighbour still makes her *kuskus* in the leisurely traditional way, sifting through it with both hands and steaming it over a vegetable stew in a special tall contraption that she calls a *kiskas* (another word that falls sweetly on my Afrikaans ear, almost like the soapbox cars we hammered together as children). This container is called a *couscoussière* – although these days all the French people I know simply buy packets of instant couscous at the supermarket, which requires no more than a kettle of boiling water.

And if this is what the French around me do, who am I to go one better? You won't find a *kiskas* in my kitchen cupboard, but there will always be, without fail, a packet of instant *kuskus* on one of the shelves. It's like olive oil – indispensable if you live anywhere near the Mediterranean.

COUSCOUS ROYAL
SERVES 8

Right: Couscous royal

It's not worth making this dish for fewer than six people – I did say that it's French bazaar food! Like any traditional stew it can be made in any number of ways. Alain was taught by our Moroccan neighbour, but changes the recipe as the spirit moves him. His advice is to listen to your inner voice until you perfect your own version.

1 chicken | 1 shoulder of lamb | 200 ml olive oil | 4 onions, finely chopped | 4 garlic cloves, finely chopped | 2 T mixed spice or ras el hanout | 200 ml tomato paste | 4 tomatoes, peeled and cubed (plunge them into boiling water for a few minutes and then rinse under the cold tap and the skin will practically fall off) | 4 carrots, sliced | 4 courgettes, sliced | 4 turnips, quartered | 2 aubergines, cubed | 1 celery stalk, cut into short lengths | 1 bunch parsley, finely chopped | 1 bouquet garni (see Indispensable on page 177) | 1 large tin chickpeas, drained | 8 merguez sausages (or any thin spicy lamb sausage) | 1 kg couscous | fresh coriander | 2 t harissa (Moroccan chilli paste) | salt and pepper

Cut the chicken into joints and the lamb shoulder into large cubes. Heat half the olive oil in a large pan and cook the onion, garlic, chicken and lamb for 15 minutes on high. Sprinkle with the spice mixture, salt and pepper. Add the tomato paste and fresh tomatoes and mix well. Add sufficient water to cover and simmer over a low heat for 30 minutes.

Add the carrots, courgettes, turnips, aubergines, celery, parsley and bouquet garni to the meat, plus more water if necessary. Bring to the boil again and simmer gently for another 30 minutes. Add the chickpeas about 5 minutes before the end.

Meanwhile pan-fry the merguez sausages and prepare the couscous with boiling water. Pour some of the remaining olive oil in a thin stream over the steaming couscous and fluff through with a fork to separate the grains. Add more olive oil if it looks a little dry.

This is one of those dishes that will have your guests falling off their chairs if you serve it with confidence and style. Heap the prepared couscous in a pile on a large flat plate and arrange the sausages in a star shape on the top. Dish the vegetables and meat into two separate bowls using a slotted spoon and garnish with finely snipped coriander leaves. Pour the sauce into a smaller bowl. Take one soup ladle of the sauce to mix with the harissa and serve this fiery little sauce separately. Smile modestly at the compliments which will inevitably follow.

TABOULÉ (TABBOULEH)

If your guests have not devoured all the semolina in your *couscous royal*, you can create a salad for another meal in a flash. On a hot day, the traditional Mediterranean *taboulé* of cold couscous mixed with good olive oil, plenty of finely chopped mint and parsley, thinly sliced tomatoes and onions, plus salt and pepper to taste is always a winner. We make our own child-friendly version by adding chunks of tuna and stirring through Alain's home-made mayonnaise. Eaten with a few slices of *pain de campagne* (a baguette made using wholemeal flour) it's always a popular lunch under the plane tree.

FOOD OF THE GODS

"IF YOU ARE NOT FEELING WELL, IF YOU HAVE NOT SLEPT, CHOCOLATE WILL REVIVE YOU. BUT YOU HAVE NO CHOCOLATE! I THINK OF THAT AGAIN AND AGAIN! MY DEAR, HOW WILL YOU EVER MANAGE?"
MADAME DE SÉVIGNÉ (1626-1696)

When I decided to begin every chapter of this book with a quotation, I realised that I might have difficulty in finding appropriate comments for courgettes, aubergines and suchlike. But chocolate, I knew, would give me no such trouble. After all, research has shown that fourteen out of every ten people like chocolate – to quote one Sandra Boynton. And all fourteen would certainly have had something memorable to say about it.

It was simply good neighbourliness that made me choose Madame de Sévigné. This formidable letter-writer died in the nearby fairy-tale castle of Grignan. Every year in July she is honoured with a *Fête de Correspondance*, a popular event at which every Tom, Dick and Harry is encouraged to sit down and write a real old-fashioned letter. On handmade paper. With a feather quill, carefully dipping it in a real inkwell. An unforgettable experience – especially for teenagers like ours whose idea of correspondence is Facebook and SMS messaging.

Down one of Grignan's cobbled streets there is also an elegant *salon de thé* with a sheltered garden next to a fountain, where I take the children sometimes to teach them that drinking tea is a ritual with a long tradition. The French are not great tea drinkers like the English, although plant-flavoured *tisanes* (tea without tannin, like our South African rooibos) are popular, especially here in the south. But you never get milk with your tea in a restaurant and when you ask for it, you often meet with a strange look – and there's a good chance that you'll be brought a jug of *hot* milk.

Luckily my friend Renée, who is also from South Africa, lives in a neighbouring town. Renée makes every cup of tea a festive occasion – and she doesn't mind if I drink mine with milk. Although the tea leaves that she keeps in a variety of tins in her cupboard – like any tea enthusiast she doesn't

believe in tea bags – often produce such irresistible aroma and taste that I forget all about adding milk. Once we've decided which tea we're going to enjoy, she brews it in a handsome teapot and then we drink it out of heirloom cups of fine bone china. Usually with something sweet, often with something chocolate. Because we both feel the deep sincerity of elegant Madame de Sévigné's *cri de coeur*. How would we ever manage without chocolate!

Another happy chance is that Renée lives next door to a bakery where we can always quickly buy a patisserie for our tea. Yet her own baking is still the most delicious. She can conjure up a milk tart that makes me weep with homesickness. On a more French note, her irresistible chocolate tart would be welcome on the smartest table as dessert. Whenever we lick the melted chocolate from our spoons, sighing in ecstasy, we understand anew why the cocoa tree's botanic name is *Theobroma cacao. Theobroma* means "food of the gods". So it wasn't nectar that sustained the gods, but chocolate. Especially the Aztec and Maya gods of Central America, where the cocoa tree grows wild. Kings and warriors in those regions had the right to drink cocoa, because it was believed to imbue them with strength and wisdom. It was however forbidden to ordinary folk – where did you ever hear of a dictator who wanted his subjects to be clever and strong? But who knows, just as Louis the Sixteenth might have been more popular if he had shared his asparagus with his people, the Meso-Americans might still be powerful nations if they'd only been a little more generous with their *theobroma*.

As Brillat-Savarin says, the fate of nations rests in the food they eat.

Please remember that next time you're looking for an excuse to go out and buy a slab of really good chocolate.

FONDANT CHOCOLAT (FRENCH CHOCOLATE TART)
SERVES 6

This is a "tart" without flour – more like a baked chocolate mousse than a cake – and with a delicious centre of melted chocolate. The word fondant has the same origin as the renowned Swiss fondue, meaning "melted"; a chocolate lover's dream.

200 g dark chocolate | 125 g butter | 150 g sugar | 6 eggs, separated | a few fresh mint leaves

Melt the chocolate and butter together in an ovenproof glass bowl over a saucepan of boiling water. (Or do it in the microwave if you're in a hurry.)

Combine the sugar and egg yolks with the melted chocolate.

Beat the egg whites until stiff. Fold gently into the other ingredients.

Spoon the mixture into a small, deep, well-buttered cake tin (or into six individual ovenproof dishes or ramekins).

Bake in a preheated oven at 200 °C for 20 minutes. After 10 minutes, cover the tart with foil to prevent it drying out. (If you're using individual dishes, reduce the overall baking time to 12 minutes.) The tart may look a little runny when you remove it from the oven, but will firm up as it cools.

Decorate with mint leaves. Then decide if you have enough patience to wait until it has cooled completely or simply eat it with a teaspoon while still lukewarm and runny.

Right: Fondant chocolat

GOOD, BETTER, BEST
If it is always important to use ingredients of the best quality when we make food, it is even more so with chocolate. The ordinary slabs that you buy at the corner café do not contain enough cocoa beans (or cocoa liquor or cocoa butter, as it is also known) to achieve the rich taste and intoxicating aroma. But if you cannot afford chocolate with 90% cocoa – and who can, these days? – you could opt for something with a lower percentage, provided it's more than 50%. (See Indispensable on page 177.)

CONCERNING COURGETTES

"What's in a name? That which we call a rose/
By any other name would smell as sweet."

William Shakespeare (1564-1616)

The courgette is a cucurbit or gourd (its engaging Latin name is *Cucurbita pepo*), which makes it a member of the Great Pumpkin family. But what has this crisp little tube with its paper-thin skin to do with the giants of its race? The pumpkin, as South African rustics know it, is a rotund, thick-skinned whopper of a vegetable, heavy enough to hold down a tin roof even when the northwesterly wind is blowing a gale.

Another more down to earth name, baby marrow, sheds some light on the connection. It's all a matter of timing. The difference lies not so much in the vegetables themselves, but when they grow and when they are harvested. Leave your courgette on the plant and it will in time expand into a hard-shelled mammoth marrow perhaps half a metre long (once a favourite subject of prize vegetable competitions).

As a rule winter-growing pumpkins and squashes are left to ripen on the plant, while summer-growing marrows are at their most delicious when picked as babies, which is usually between 6 cm and 10 cm for courgettes, and no more than 5 cm for patty pans.

So this little green finger may be no more than a baby marrow, but it is one of the giants of Provençal and Mediterranean cuisine – imagine a ratatouille or a tian without courgettes!

The Americans have confused things even more by giving the baby marrow another exotic name, zucchini. (Every word that begins with a "z" always sounds exotic, except if you're Polish.) All this is enough to make me exclaim, as Romeo to his Juliet: *"What's in a name?"* A marrow is a courgette is a summer squash is a zucchini – by any other name as sweet, as delicious.

And while we're on the subject of flowers, it's good to know that the beautiful golden yellow flower of the summer squash is also a prized delicacy. My feminist friends are of the opinion that these flowers can also teach us a lesson. The female flower is simply there to attract insects. Once pollinated it fades and withers as the courgette begins to grow. In contrast the male flower grows larger and lovelier and more golden, but never becomes anything more than a flower. I'm not absolutely sure what the moral of the story is, but I think it's something to do with vainglorious display versus noble self-sacrifice.

Before my men friends become annoyed, let me immediately say that the most delicious courgette flowers I have ever eaten were prepared by a male chef. It's a dish that we never make ourselves, because it's difficult to find the flowers unless you grow your own – and probably also because our Italian neighbours do it so much better. Our local Italian, Armando, is a master flower chef. When I received my first invitation to a flower braai, I realised just how far away I was from my Afrikaans roots. My uncles and cousins will barely eat a leaf, as in lettuce, with their braaivleis. I can hardly imagine their faces, if instead of meat, they were offered flowers!

Baby marrows, like tomatoes, are a summer vegetable that has become available throughout the year, and so at times are of indifferent quality. And like tomatoes (or any other fruit or vegetable), they are best eaten in the season when nature intended them to grow and even better if they've been grown nearby and not spoiled by a long journey. If you live just this side of the North Pole or in a desert, you will naturally have to lower your standards. But the rest of us ought always to aim for the very best possible flavour when we eat fruit and vegetables. As Oscar Wilde put it: *"I have but the simplest taste. I am always satisfied with the best."*

WHAT IS A GRATIN?

Nowadays most of us think of a gratin as a baked dish covered with a layer of cheese or crumbs. But originally the word simply referred to the tasty crust that remained behind in the dish once the contents had vanished – that crust always seized upon, scratched out and devoured by the greediest person at the table. The French word for scratch is *gratter*. And that's why a gratin always comes to the table in its baking dish – otherwise no one can *gratter* the gratin!

BABY MARROW MOUSSE
SERVES 4

Children are usually not mad about courgettes unless cunningly disguised. Here is a recipe for wily mums, lazy cooks and busy hosts (it can be made the day before). It quickly became one of my daughter's favourite foods, so much so that she recently chose it for her birthday lunch above pasta and pizza!

2 small courgettes | 2 T pesto (bought pesto is good, home-made better, see page 177) | 60 g grated Parmesan cheese | 1 T crème fraîche (thick slightly sour cream) | 20 g pine nuts | a few fresh basil leaves | salt and pepper

Cut the courgettes into chunks and steam for a few minutes, making sure they stay crisp.

Drain well and combine in a food processor with the pesto, Parmesan and crème fraîche. Aim for a mousse with a chunky texture. Add salt and pepper to taste. Spoon into a bowl, cover with clingfilm and chill.

Just before serving, toast the pine nuts in a non-stick pan until golden, turning them several times. Dish the cold mousse into four bowls and sprinkle with the pine nuts and snipped basil leaves. Serve cold with slices of ham or smoked salmon or a beef carpaccio. It can also be stirred into hot pasta as you would pesto.

PETIT GRATIN DE COURGETTE
SERVES 4

2 firm, fairly large courgettes | 4 eggs | 2 fresh garlic cloves, crushed | 3 T crème fraîche | 150 ml milk | fresh thyme leaves and flowers | butter, salt and pepper

Slice the courgettes very thinly and arrange over the bottom and sides of a well-buttered flan tin (or use four individual ovenproof dishes or ramekins). Beat the eggs in a bowl with the garlic, crème fraîche, milk and thyme leaves. Season with salt and pepper and pour into the flan tin or divide among the four dishes or ramekins.

Bake in a preheated oven at 180 °C for about 15 minutes until the egg mixture is cooked but still moist. (Reduce the baking time to 10 minutes if you're using individual dishes.) Garnish with thyme flowers and eat at once.

Right: Petit gratin de courgette

THREE CHEERS FOR CHICKEN

"I WANT THERE TO BE NO PEASANT IN MY KINGDOM SO POOR THAT HE CANNOT HAVE A CHICKEN IN HIS POT EVERY SUNDAY."

HENRI IV OF FRANCE (1553-1610)

The French, like the English, have had a whole string of Henrys as king. Henry the Fourth (Henri Quatre), who expressed the famous wish above, was the most popular of the lot. When he came to the throne many of his subjects were so poor that they could not afford even a mouthful of chicken, but four centuries later, the French have become formidable meat eaters – almost the equal of my uncles on the South African platteland, I sometimes think. Nevertheless, Henri's "chicken in the pot" remains a popular choice for Sunday lunch.

Today though, the chicken is more usually roasted in an oven than cooked in a pot and often eaten with the universal *frites* (fried chips), a meal most certainly unknown to the sixteenth century peasant.

To me the most interesting thing about King Henri's words is that they are almost always translated incorrectly, because he spoke of a hen in the pot *(poule au pot)*, not any genderless old chicken. The English may believe that a rose is a rose is a rose, but for a Frenchman a chicken is never just a chicken. *Non, non, non.* For some dishes, such as *coq au vin*, you must have a rooster. My gentle Alain can become quite rude when he comes across recipes in Anglo-Saxon cookbooks for *coq au vin* made with generic factory chickens. "*Putain!* The recipe is called cock with wine, not chicken with wine!" The dish apparently evolved as a way of dealing with stringy old farmyard roosters; only a grandfather cock could be stewed long enough for the wine to be thoroughly absorbed without the meat disintegrating from the bones.

The same explanation goes more or less for *poule au pot*. In the days when everyone kept chickens, there were various ways of cooking old hens economically but tastily. The longer granny can stay simmering in the pot, the better she will taste. And if you think an aged fowl boiled in water with a few herbs sounds as unappetising as boiled shoe leather, well, I must admit I thought the same. Until I tasted my mother-in-law's *poule au pot*.

Sometimes the sex of the chicken is less important than its place of origin. The "tricolour" *poularde de Bresse* remains the supreme chicken – the head boasts a bright red comb, the skin is beautifully white and the black feet have a blue sheen – the three colours of the French flag, in fact. These *poulardes* are sold with feet and head still attached and are the only chickens to carry the country's flag as their official seal of quality.

But these aristocrats are by no means the only high-class chickens in the land. (The fact that the French chose a rooster as a symbol for their rugby team, should be a fair indication of the esteem in which poultry is held here.) Almost as much in demand are the yellow and black chickens of Challans; yellow because the skin is a golden colour, black once again because of the feet. And if you cannot afford the pricey poultry of Bresse or Challans, you can still buy succulent farm chickens from Gers or Landes. I must admit that it sometimes amuses me, this obsession with the right chicken for the right recipe, but it does speak volumes about the respect with which food is still treated in my adopted country.

If even "ordinary" farm chickens are too expensive for you – often the case for a large family like ours – you can still feast on a modest "factory chicken" cooked with a little inspiration. Towards the end of the month, we often buy a generic, sexless, cheap *poulet* and doctor it with fresh herbs or an indecent amount of garlic until it tastes almost aristocratic. And on a Sunday afternoon, as we sit and suck the sweet garlic cloves, we wonder if old Henri Quatre could ever have dreamed just how much of a blessing his *poule au pot* would become to an ordinary French family.

SUNDAY'S CHICKEN IN THE POT (POULE AU POT)

If you can get hold of an old hen, count your blessings and proceed as follows: Boil 2 litres of water in a pot and add the chicken, together with 2 carrots, an onion stuck with a few cloves, and a bouquet garni (see page 177). Simmer for at least 2 hours, perhaps longer, until tender. Just before serving, make a brown sauce by combining a little flour and butter over a low heat and stirring in half a glass of the bouillon in which the chicken was cooked. If the mysteries of brown sauce are unknown to you, ask your mother or grandmother or a seasoned cook to show you how. Then you need to add some acidity to the sauce. Either, as my mother-in-law in northern France does, by adding a few splashes of vinegar and a handful of finely chopped gherkins, or, like my neighbour here in the south, with the juice of half a lemon and 2 tablespoons of capers. Grind over salt and pepper to taste and serve each guest with a portion of chicken and rice, topped with the deliciously tart sauce.

CHICKEN WITH 40 CLOVES OF GARLIC
SERVES 6

Few people have not heard of this recipe, but many have not had the courage to try it. If you are addicted to garlic, you can simply put the unpeeled cloves into the chicken cavity and roast it in the oven, but if you are uncertain as to whether your guests or your children will appreciate that much garlic, do try this more sophisticated version of Sunday's "chicken in the pot". With the addition of cream and alcohol the garlic becomes sweet and very tasty.

3-4 heads of garlic (about 40 cloves) | 1 large chicken, jointed (or buy 6 separate joints) | 1 T butter | 2 T olive oil | 3 T cognac (or good brandy) | 1½ cups of dry white wine | 2 T fresh thyme leaves (or sage or parsley, as long as it's fresh) | 2 T flour | 3 T crème fraîche | salt and pepper

Break up the heads of garlic and plunge the cloves into boiling water for a minute. Drain and peel. If you make the dish in summer with young garlic, you can use the cloves whole; if not, halve the "old garlic" (*ail sec*) and remove the green shoot, otherwise the garlic will taste bitter.

Season the chicken on both sides with freshly ground salt and pepper. Heat the butter and oil in a heavy-based pot over a medium to high heat. Brown the chicken portions for about 4 minutes on each side until golden brown. Remove and set aside.

Add the garlic cloves to the pot, reduce the heat and stir-fry for about 7 minutes until evenly browned. Add 2 tablespoons of the cognac and the wine and raise the heat until the liquid comes to the boil. Scrape the pot to loosen the brown bits. Return the chicken to the pot together with the thyme leaves. Cover and allow to simmer over a low heat for about 30 minutes until tender. Remove the chicken, cover with foil and keep warm.

Remove half a cup of liquid from the pot, combine with the flour in a small bowl, and stir into the liquid in the pot. Raise the heat, add the remaining cognac and the crème fraîche and cook for 3 minutes. Season to taste with salt and pepper. Spoon the sauce and the garlic cloves over the chicken and serve immediately.

Right: Chicken with 40 cloves of garlic

TURNING OVER A NEW LEAF

"THE FIRST GATHERINGS OF THE GARDEN IN MAY OF SALADS, RADISHES
AND HERBS MADE ME FEEL LIKE A MOTHER ABOUT HER BABY – HOW COULD
ANYTHING SO BEAUTIFUL BE MINE."

ALICE B TOKLAS (1877-1967)

Every Frenchman knows his salads, according to Brillat-Savarin. As proof he offers an amusing little anecdote regarding a certain D'Albignac who fled to London during the Revolution and made a very comfortable living there by making salads and salad dressings for wealthy English households. This fashionable salad maker, as the noble Frenchman was described, drew on an ever-widening range of seasonings and ingredients – *"vinegars with different scents, oils with or without fruit flavours, soya, caviar, truffles, anchovies,"* to name but a few.

I am not French, but during the last decade I have learnt to do many things with leaves and dressings and seasonings. My daughter calls me *La Reine de Salade* – the Queen of Salad – although she would probably prefer to have a Queen of Cake for a mother. She refuses to eat leaves, but one day she may well discover what she has been missing. I also detested leaves when I was small – and now I sing songs of praise daily to these green miracles.

Sometimes I yearn for a particular kind of leaf, say rocket or watercress, and I recall with renewed respect the ancient fairy tale of Rapunzel. Rapunzel owed her name to her mother's desperate hankering for lamb's lettuce when she was pregnant. The lamb's lettuce (*Rapunze* in German) grew only in the garden of a powerful witch, but Rapunzel's mother persuaded her husband that she would die if she could not have some of those succulent green leaves to eat. What could the poor man do but go and steal the leaves? Of course the witch caught him and in his terror he promised to give her the child that was soon to be born ...

Do read this delightful tale again – and remember, the next time you nibble on this modest little leaf, that it must be one of the few greens that has inspired the creation of a world famous storybook character.

The secret of a successful green salad lies in knowing your leaves. This may sound obvious, but ask around and you'll soon realise that many people stick to the predictable iceberg lettuce simply because they don't know enough about all the other salad leaves. You need, for instance, to know that the leaves of butter lettuces are as soft as a baby's skin, with a delicate flavour, and that cos lettuce, the one with leaves erect around its stalk, has a subtle bite and is most often used in the classic Caesar salad. You need to know that rocket is actually a herb with a firm texture and a sharp, peppery flavour, while the softer leaves of watercress are more mustardy on the tongue. And that corn salad is soft and mild enough for lambs, as indicated by its popular name lamb's lettuce.

It's also good to know that the ruffled edges of frisée look lovely in any salad bowl and do not wilt as easily as other less robust leaves when you drizzle a warm dressing over them. Among the more unusual leaves, red radicchio and the beautiful endive (also known as chicory) are both bitter and delicious, or simply delicious, and also perfectly suited to warm dressings. Also keep in mind that there are various kinds of spinach that will lend an appealing dark green and a surprising texture to other leaves – and that edible flowers like nasturtiums add a wonderful spark of colour to the simplest salad. And then there are all the herbs – basil, mint, chervil, fennel, coriander and many, many others – which can lift a basic salad from humdrum to heavenly.

I like to arrange a salad of leaves, flowers and herbs in a huge serving dish in the centre of the table. It provides a striking table decoration, more original than the usual bunch of flowers, and it amuses me to watch everyone devour the decoration.

SALADS WITH SEEDS

Add zing to a simple green salad by adding a variety of roasted nuts and/or seeds. Scatter almond flakes, pine nuts and sunflower seeds (or hazelnuts, pieces of walnut, sesame seeds or whatever you have to hand) on a baking sheet. Slide the pan under a preheated grill for 2-3 minutes, turning the nuts and seeds regularly until they are golden brown. Remove from the heat and allow to cool. Sprinkle the nuts over a mixture of bitter leaves such as chicory, frisée and radicchio and drizzle with nutty salad dressing (recipe below) or a vinaigrette of your choice.

Right: Nutty salad dressing

WARM CHORIZO SALAD
SERVES 4

250 g "strong" salad leaves (such as endive/chicory, frisée, radicchio) | a handful of sage leaves | 5 T olive oil | 300 g Spanish chorizo sausage, thinly sliced (or salami slices sprinkled with a little mild chilli powder) | 1 small red onion, thinly sliced | 1 garlic clove, finely chopped | 2 T red wine vinegar | salt and pepper

Arrange the salad leaves on a large platter and scatter with the sage leaves. Heat the olive oil in a pan and fry the chorizo for a minute on a high heat. Add the onion and garlic and fry for another 2-3 minutes or until the chorizo is brown and crisp. Remove the pan from the heat, stir in the vinegar and season with salt and pepper.

Pour this warm dressing over the leaves, toss quickly and serve immediately.

NUTTY SALAD DRESSING
MAKES ABOUT 150 ML

3 T balsamic vinegar (or Banyuls or sherry vinegar) | 1 t brown sugar | 1 t Dijon mustard | 125 ml walnut oil (or hazelnut oil) | 1 T finely chopped walnuts (or hazelnuts) | 1 T fresh parsley, finely chopped (or another herb such as basil, thyme or sage, as long as it's fresh) | salt and pepper

Combine the vinegar, sugar and mustard in a small bowl. Grind over salt and pepper to taste. Whisk in the oil and finally stir in the nuts and herbs.

Drizzle over a leaf salad with roasted nuts. This dressing will also liven up a simple green salad or even a plain potato salad.

LEAVES WITH A KICK

If you add spices to the nuts before you roast them, the salad will have even more zing. Again, use almonds, pecans, walnuts, pine nuts, whichever you fancy. Stir-fry for a minute in a little butter to which you have added a teaspoon of Worcestershire sauce, a teaspoon of mild chilli powder, a pinch of ground cumin and salt and pepper. Transfer to a baking sheet and place under a preheated grill for about 7 minutes. Turn regularly and remove from the heat when the nuts or seeds are an even golden brown. This time, mix sweet and peppery leaves in a large bowl, for example rocket and corn salad, spinach and chervil (see page 177) – the more leaves, the merrier. Also add some chopped chives or spring onions. Drizzle with a classic French vinaigrette (see page 177) and scatter with the spiced nuts and seeds.

OILS AND VINEGARS

As the noble D'Albignac knew long ago, oils and vinegars of different flavours are indispensable to the fashionable salad maker. Our larder always contains Italian balsamic and often French Banyuls vinegar, good wine vinegar, apple cider vinegar and at least one herbed vinegar such as tarragon.

When it comes to oils, we use the best pure virgin olive oil that we can afford, as well as nutty oils such as walnut, hazelnut and sesame oil. And we usually have a small bottle of truffle oil to hand for those days when we're in lavish mood. A few drops can transform a cheap cauliflower soup into a dish for a millionaire. A real case of saucery!

THE NAMING OF DISHES

"ONE CANNOT THINK WELL, LOVE WELL, SLEEP WELL, IF ONE HAS NOT DINED WELL."

VIRGINIA WOOLF (1882–1941)

Tian always sounds to me like an Afrikaans rugby player – but it's really the name of a traditional Provençal vegetable dish. And it's made with the same ingredients as that more renowned, even more peculiarly named Provençal dish, ratatouille.

Thanks to an animated film from America, children all over the world now know what ratatouille is. Many of them have even learnt to *eat* ratatouille. Ratatouille the film star rat also succeeded in explaining to my daughter the fundamental principle of gastronomic pleasure. You taste something that you like and it explodes like a cracker on your tongue. You taste something else you like and there's another bang. Then you combine the two ingredients, eat them together and – *voilà!* – a whole fireworks performance for your taste buds.

Merci, Ratatouille. Now I'm waiting for the Americans to make a child-friendly movie about tian, because for me it is even more tasty than ratatouille. Although my husband is of the opinion that the dish served in Ratatouille's restaurant is in any event a tian!

For both dishes, each kind of vegetable is cooked separately, in a saucepan on the stove. It's true that some cooks mix the vegetables for ratatouille from the beginning, but then you might just as well go and buy the tinned version, according to my husband. (Personally, I rather like tinned ratatouille, especially when you see how long it takes to cook "real" ratatouille, but naturally this is sacrilege as far as the Frenchman in my house is concerned.) The difference is that for a ratatouille, you mix all the vegetables at the end – which is what the French word *touiller* means – whereas for a tian you arrange the sautéed vegetables in layers and bake them in the oven. And this is a Very Important Difference.

It means that the layer-by-layer ratatouilles of famous food writers like Julia Child, which some cooks also shove into the oven – *quelle horreur!* – do not meet my husband's strict requirements. I would rather not argue with him. He was born in France and has lived for years in Provence. For him, unlike Julia Child, ratatouille is a matter of honour. National, provincial and personal honour.

So let me stick to less debatable information. The original Provençal name for ratatouille was *ratatolha* – the French *touiller* is related to "toss" in English – while tian originally referred to a shallow earthenware dish in which vegetables were baked. Gradually the name of the dish became the name of its contents – as happened with the Moroccan tagine.

By this time it should be clear that discussion of the food of Provence is difficult without bringing in the centuries-old language of the region. When the ancient Romans were driven back over the Alps, two languages developed simultaneously in France: Oïl in the north and Oc in the south. The names are derived from the words for "yes". (The word *oïl* gradually became the modern French *oui*.)

Oc was spoken over a wide area, Occitania (which included Provence), and was known as the language of the troubadours of the south, the poetic language of courtly love. In the sixteenth century an edict was issued which made the prosaic northern form of French the official language of administration and trade. From then on Oc or Provençal was looked upon as an unsophisticated rural dialect – until Frédéric Mistral, winner of the Nobel Prize for Literature in 1904, brought the language of the troubadours to life again. It's ironic that the more business-like northern French is today marketed worldwide as the romantic language of love while the truly romantic language of Provence lives on virtually only in gastronomy.

But then you could certainly argue that any language involved in cookery will always be a language of love. Doesn't the way to the heart lie through the stomach? As far as I'm concerned, as long as my Frenchman continues to feed me fragrant Provençal dishes like tian and ratatouille, I shall continue to sing the praises of love *and* of the lovely language of Provence.

TIAN

SERVES 4-6

6 T olive oil | 2 onions, finely chopped | 4 garlic cloves, finely chopped | 1 aubergine, sliced (you can salt it – see Indispensable on page 179) | 2 sweet red peppers, seeded and cut into strips | 2 large courgettes, sliced | 3 large tomatoes, sliced | sprigs of fresh thyme and rosemary | 3 T fresh white bread-crumbs | 2 T grated Parmesan cheese | salt and pepper

Heat 4 tablespoons of olive oil in a large pan and fry the onions, garlic, aubergine and red pepper until golden brown. Remove with a slotted spoon and spread the mixture over the bottom of a shallow ovenproof dish. Fry the courgette slices in the same oil for about a minute on each side, just long enough to soften them.

Arrange a row of tomato slices on top of the vegetable mixture in the dish; each tomato slice must overlap the previous one slightly. Arrange a row of courgette slices in the same way alongside, then another row of tomato slices, alternating until the mixture is completely covered. Grind over salt and pepper and scatter with sprigs of rosemary and thyme.

Bake in a preheated oven at 190 °C for 25 minutes or until golden brown. Remove the dish from the oven and scatter with the breadcrumbs and cheese. If the top layer of vegetables looks dry, drizzle with a trickle of olive oil. Bake for another 10 minutes until the layer of breadcrumbs becomes crisp and golden brown.

Serve immediately, or an hour later, or the next day as a picnic meal. A tian is one of those wonderful dishes that remains delicious whether piping hot, lukewarm or cold.

RATATOUILLE

SERVES 6

1 kg tomatoes | 125 ml olive oil | 500 g aubergine, cubed | 500 g courgettes, sliced | 500 g onions, finely chopped | 500 g green peppers (or a mixture of red and green), seeded and cut into strips | 5 garlic cloves, finely chopped | sprigs of fresh rosemary, thyme and marjoram | fresh basil and parsley | salt and pepper

Plunge the tomatoes into boiling water for a few minutes. Remove, peel and cut into chunks.

Heat half the oil in a heavy-based saucepan. Add the aubergine cubes and stir-fry gently over a medium heat until golden brown. Add the courgettes and cook for about 5 minutes, or until they colour. Remove the vegetables with a slotted spoon and set aside.

Pour the remaining oil into the saucepan. Add the onions and stir-fry until soft and golden. Add the peppers and the garlic, turn up the heat and cook for 3-4 minutes. Add the tomatoes and cook for another 10 minutes.

Add the aubergine and the courgettes to the rest of the vegetables, season with salt and pepper and snipped leaves of rosemary, thyme and marjoram. Simmer with the lid off, over a medium to low heat for 30 minutes. Garnish with basil and parsley and eat hot or cold.

Right: Tian

ON LOVE APPLES AND WOLF PEACHES

"You like tomato and I like tomahto. / Potato, potahto, tomato, tomahto, / Let's call the whole thing off."

Ira Gershwin (1896-1983)

The tomato is both wonderful and confusing. One, there is the vexed question of pronunciation (tomahto/tomayto), a cause of vehement differences of opinion. Two, most of us know that the tomato is actually a fruit – belonging to the berry family, to be precise – but we continue to think of it as a vegetable. We look for it among other vegetables at the market – and find it with the leeks and potatoes rather than the apples and pears. And in the kitchen we use it as a vegetable.

And how we use it! It's hard to believe that the ubiquitous tomato, without which it would be virtually impossible to cook in Provence and other Mediterranean regions, was until relatively recently regarded as deadly poisonous. Yet another misconception in the history of this delightful vegetable. I mean this fantastic fruit.

A Frenchman is at least partly to blame for this particular mix-up. When the botanist Tournefort coined the tomato's Latin name (*Lycopersicon esculentum* – which may be translated as "wolf peach"), he apparently confused the tomato with a poisonous fruit which had been used centuries earlier to get rid of wolves. And until the nineteenth century many people believed that a single bite would be enough to kill you, just like Snow White and the witch's apple.

The comparison with apples is not coincidental. The Italians christened tomatoes *pomi d'oro* or "golden apples", apparently because the first importations from Central America to Europe were yellow in colour. And the French referred to *pommes d'amour* or "love apples" – because they believed that tomatoes had exciting, erotic properties – but then what else would you expect from the French? A true Frenchman would probably be able to discern erotic properties in beans or cauliflowers.

As always when it comes to food, the French believe that every tomato should know its place. Or every cook should know his tomatoes. Just as you wouldn't slaughter any old chicken for *poule au pot*, you wouldn't use just any tomato for a salad, a tart or a soup. Small cherry tomatoes, firm as a young man's butt, look lovely in a mixed salad or a flan. Medium-sized tomatoes, bumpy on the outside, juicy within, are like plain girls: you soon realise that character counts for more than looks. These are the ones for a soup or a sauce (the tomatoes, not the girls). And when you get really huge, heavyweight tomatoes, you make *tomates farcies*, another Provençal classic.

When the soup king Joseph Campbell introduced tomato soup in tins in 1897, this fruit pretending to be a vegetable became even more popular. You only have to think of Andy Warhol's famous series of screen prints. The artist originally depicted all 32 kinds of soup canned by Campbell's in the sixties – but it was the tomato soup that became an icon. The high acidity of tomatoes makes them particularly suitable for canning and even those of us who abominate tinned food will seldom be found without a tin of tomatoes or tomato purée in our grocery cupboards.

In any dish, fresh tomatoes are always better, but they must be real, fresh tomatoes and not the tasteless, factory-farmed objects that you find in supermarkets throughout the year. If a tomato doesn't smell like a tomato, you might as well go and buy it in a tin. Freshly picked, their scent is one of the most evocative on earth, laden with sunshine and summer, the generosity of the soil and the promise of delicious pleasure. Now that I think of it again, it's no wonder that the French called these juicy red fruits "love apples" …

FARCIS PROVENÇAUX
SERVES 6

Right: Farcis Provençaux

Farci usually refers to vegetables that have been hollowed out and filled with a savoury mixture of meat or rice and vegetables. Sometimes we use only tomatoes, but if you have onion and aubergine to add, the filling is even tastier. Traditionally, minced pork or a mixture of veal and pork is used, making the filling appealingly light in colour, but we have also made it quite successfully with beef.

6 large tomatoes | 2 large aubergines | 2 large onions | 7 T olive oil | salt and pepper

FILLING
375 g mincemeat (pork or veal) | 1 onion, finely chopped | 2 garlic cloves, finely crushed | a handful of chopped parsley | 2 T grated Parmesan cheese | 2 T boiled rice | the leaves off 2 sprigs of thyme | 2 eggs, beaten | salt and pepper

Slice the top off each tomato, scoop out the flesh and set aside. Cut the aubergines in half lengthwise, hollow out and set the flesh aside. Plunge the onions into boiling water for 1-2 minutes, then drain. Cut the tops off. Hollow out and add the flesh to the tomato and aubergine. Sprinkle salt, pepper and a little olive oil into each vegetable shell.

For the filling, combine the mince, onion, garlic, parsley and vegetable pulp in a bowl. Heat a tablespoon of olive oil in a pan and cook the filling over a low heat for about 5 minutes, stirring continuously.

Remove the pan from the heat and stir in the cheese, rice, thyme and beaten egg. Add salt and pepper to taste.

Arrange the vegetable shells in two large ovenproof dishes and divide the filling between them. Sprinkle with the remaining olive oil and bake in a preheated oven at 180 °C for 45 minutes. If the vegetables begin to look dry during baking, baste them with a little more olive oil. They must shine when you take them out of the oven.

Serve every guest with a glistening whole tomato, half an aubergine and if they wish, a whole or half an onion. Serve with steaming hot white rice.

CLASSIC SIMPLICITY
On a hot summer's day a basic tomato salad is delicious proof that simple dishes often provide the greatest gastronomic pleasure. Slice ripe red, fragrant tomatoes and arrange in concentric circles on a large platter. Drizzle with the best olive oil in the house, add enough salt and a few turns of pepper, plus a handful of torn basil leaves. Because we live where we do, we usually add a few shiny black Nyons olives – also because they look so beautiful with the red and the green. Most important: let the salad rest in the fridge for at least 15 minutes so that the juice of the tomatoes has time to combine with the other flavours. Serve with a wholemeal baguette to soak up every last drop of this tasty juice from your plate.

STUMBLING ON MELONS

"FRIENDS ARE LIKE MELONS; SHALL I TELL YOU WHY?
TO FIND ONE GOOD YOU MUST ONE HUNDRED TRY."

CLAUDE MERMET (CIRCA 1550-1605)

A ccording to Mermet's original French maxim you must try no less than fifty melons – or friends – to find one good one. In the English translation the number has doubled, which perhaps merely indicates that in France it's easier to find outstanding melons, if not outstanding friends.

Two hundred years after Mermet, the American Benjamin Franklin gloomily declared that "men and melons are hard to know". Now, thanks to modern transport and cultivation methods, it's become less of a trial than in the days of Mermet and Franklin to find a perfectly sweet and juicy melon. And yet the French Charentais melon remains world famous for its exotically sweet, almost musky flavour and soft, bright orange flesh that you can eat right down to the rind. Even in Frances Case's hugely entertaining guide *1001 Foods You Must Try Before You Die*, this French melon is chosen above the Italian cantaloupe from which it was originally bred.

As luck would have it, most Charentais melons are grown around Cavaillon, a mere stone's throw from where we live in the north of Provence. It's fair to say that our family regards it as a patriotic duty to consume as many of these magnificent melons as we possibly can each summer. And just in case you think that I'm overstating the glory of our region – can one family of gourmands get that lucky? – I call as my witness for the defence one Alexandre Dumas, author of *The Three Musketeers*.

Yes, the man behind Athos, Porthos and Aramis was born in Cavaillon and raised on melon juice. When his fame had spread far and wide, he was asked to donate a complete set of his works to the town library of his birthplace. Because he was a prolific writer, this meant an enormous gift of more than 400 books. Dumas agreed, on one condition: that he would be sent an annual consignment of Cavaillon's melons for the rest of his life.

Now do you believe me when I boast about these beauties of the region?

It's true that it is still not easy to tell precisely when even the best melon is ripe enough to eat. Here in our town Madame Voisine believes that scent is the first and most important indication. She sniffs each melon at the market as a wine buff would a glass of Gigondas or Vacqueras from our Côtes du Rhône. Once her nose has detected a whiff of ripeness, she feels carefully around the stem for that almost undetectable yielding of the rind. "*Voilà!*" Madame Voisine sighs, eyes closed in bliss. "*Un bon melon.*"

When I see her and the other women of the town so absorbed in front of a pile of melons, I am almost moved to poetry. Then I understand what Andrew Marvell was getting at when he wrote: "*Fair quiet, have I found thee here | And innocence thy sister dear? … Stumbling on melons, as I pass, | Ensnared with flowers, I fall on grass.*" I imagine myself tripping over melons sweet as honey, delightful as first love, and there and then, I buy a melon and carry it home as an offering to my grateful family.

MELON IN A GLASS
SERVES 6

Everyone is probably familiar with cubes of melon wrapped in slivers of Parma ham or *jambon cru* and garnished with mint. Surprise your guests with this more original starter in a glass.

2 melons | 300 g gorgonzola cheese | a handful of chopped basil leaves | 4 T olive oil | salt and pepper

Chill the melons in the fridge for at least 12 hours. Cut the gorgonzola into cubes. Make balls of melon with an ice cream spoon, or cut out flatter chunks with a soup spoon.

Combine the melon with the gorgonzola and basil leaves, drizzle with olive oil and season with salt and pepper.

Spoon the mixture into pretty glasses, decorate each with a whole basil leaf and serve at once, while the melon is still deliciously cool.

Right: Melon in a glass

MELON LIBATION
When summer festivals are held in our town square, with dozens of guests at long tables, we are often served melon as a starter, prepared in the easiest way possible. Each guest is served a chilled half melon, with pips removed and a glass of golden Beaumes de Venise poured into the hollow. The melon is bathed in the sweet, cold wine as you carve it out by the spoonful and slurp it up along with the wine. In South Africa you can substitute a chilled dessert wine for the Beaumes de Venise – and, with just a little imagination, the cicadas of Provence will sing for you.

MELON SOUP, FORSOOTH
Here is a refreshing summer soup that combines two renowned flavours of the south: Cavaillon's melons and the pastis of Marseille. I myself am not a pastis drinker, so I sometimes replace the pastis and the fennel in this recipe with vodka and nasturtium flowers. (You then lose the characteristic aniseed flavour, of course.) In a blender combine 3 melons with 3 tablespoons pastis, 6 ice cubes, salt and pepper. Use a fourth melon to cut out cubes or balls with a round spoon. Add these to the liquid and chill in the fridge. Serve in glasses or soup plates and garnish with sprigs of fennel. *Santé!*

FULL OF BEANS

"I WAS DETERMINED TO KNOW BEANS."
HENRY DAVID THOREAU (1817-1862)

Until I found myself in France, I was so accustomed to beans in dried or tinned form that I had almost completely forgotten that they could be fresh. Excepting, of course, the green beans that we ate as children – often cooked to death, alas – in green bean bredie, that favourite standby of many a mother.

Here I got to know a range of *haricots* as wide as heaven's mercy, from green to white to speckled to the prettiest little pink ones, known as *coco rose*. Among the green beans there are long, thin ones that taste delicious in salads and their more thickset aunts, which are better sliced or shredded and used in bredies.

The lovely pale green flageolet with its creamy flavour, sometimes called the Rolls-Royce of beans, is a distant relative. In France the flageolet is traditionally served with roast lamb – which, according to generations of seriously committed diners, is a culinary marriage made in heaven.

Among the other colours you have the earthy and unpretentious broad or field bean – if the flageolet is a Rolls, then the broad bean is a Volkswagen. Then there is the blond butter bean, a modest freckled one, the name of which I can never remember, and the fat *fève*, traditionally hidden in tarts as a good luck charm.

Beans are so plentiful in this country that you quickly realise why the long green ones are simply called French beans – although they, like all beans, came originally from Central America. The word *haricot* is derived from the Aztec *ayecotl*, a fact of which most French cooks are probably unaware. But what they do know is that beans are an indispensable ingredient in many French dishes that have become world famous, from a simple *salade niçoise* with green beans, lettuce leaves, tomatoes, black olives, hardboiled eggs, tuna and anchovies to the complicated cassoulets of Toulouse.

French or not, green beans were never a favourite in our house – until in China, of all places, I discovered the most delicious green beans I had ever tasted. They were meant to be a side dish, one of many set out on the table in delicate little bowls meant to be shared with other guests, but this particular garlic-suffused bowl I wiped clean all by myself. Back at home I tried the dish out at once on my family. The children were mad about it – even Mia, who at that stage was refusing to eat anything green.

But the very best thing that you can do with a selection of fresh beans, is to make a traditional Provençal *soupe au pistou*. For everyone with roots or branches in Provence, this is the soup that evokes summer days. The hum of cicadas, the metallic clink of petanque balls, the scent of lavender and pastis, the leafy cool of plane trees.

For me, part of the enjoyment of *pistou* lies in the pleasurable search for suitable beans at the morning market. The first time, I was stupid enough to ask the burly woman behind the table how much of each kind of bean I should buy for my soup, which almost led to civil war. When the vegetable seller advised me to buy equal amounts of white, red and green beans, a little old lady on my left nearly had a fit. "*Non! Non!*" she protested, *pistou* soup demanded more white and red beans, fewer green. And don't forget the *fèves*, chipped in another, otherwise your soup won't be worth eating. "*Quoi?*" cried the little old lady indignantly. She had made *soupe au pistou* for decades without *fèves*! When someone else said that her grandmother would leave out the green beans, tempers flared so frighteningly that I fled – without a single bean. This is one of those dangerous dishes, I realised, for which every cook has a recipe that has been in the family for generations. So I phoned my mother-in-law for advice, and learnt to buy my beans in silence.

STIR-FRIED BEANS WITH GARLIC

All you need is a pile of fine green beans (the fresher the better), 2-3 cloves of garlic, a little olive oil and soya sauce. Shred the beans and chop the garlic finely. Heat the oil in a wok or large frying pan. (If you don't have a wok, think seriously about buying one. Once you begin cooking in it you will wonder how you ever managed without one.) Stir-fry the beans for a few minutes while you add a few splashes of soya sauce to taste. Add the garlic and stir-fry for another minute or two. The garlic must not brown and the beans should still be crisp when you remove them from the heat. Season with coarsely ground black pepper – and prepare to be amazed when your children fall upon their greens and devour them.

SOUPE AU PISTOU

SERVES 6

Right: Soupe au pistou

If green beans are the only fresh ones available, you can use dried white and red beans, which must be soaked overnight. The soup will still be enjoyable, thanks to the *pistou*, and you will at least not find yourself involved in a bean barney at your local market.

2-3 T olive oil | 1 onion, finely chopped | 2 leeks, sliced | 4 carrots, peeled and sliced | 4 potatoes, peeled and sliced | 250 g broad beans or butter beans | 250 g red or speckled beans | 250 g green beans, cut into pieces | 100 g fèves or flageolet beans or any others (optional) | 6 tomatoes, peeled and cubed | 2 celery stalks, cut into pieces | 4 courgettes | 1 bouquet garni (see page 177) | pistou (made from garlic, basil, olive oil and Parmesan cheese – recipe on page 177) | salt and pepper

Heat the olive oil in a heavy-based pot and fry the onion gently until transparent. Add the leeks, carrots and potatoes and fry for 2-3 minutes over a medium heat. Add water to cover so that the flavours can begin to develop. After a few minutes add the other vegetables gradually in layers, for example a layer of green beans, a layer of tomatoes, a layer of white beans, a layer of celery and so on until the last layer, which should be the whole courgettes. After each layer, add more water to cover. Add the bouquet garni, salt and pepper, cover and allow to simmer over a low heat.

After 45 minutes remove the lid and mash the courgettes with a fork – the pulp will help to bind the soup. At the same time check to see if the beans are cooked. As soon as they are tender but still slightly crunchy, remove the pot from the heat.

Remove the bouquet garni and stir in 2-3 tablespoons *pistou* before you take the soup to the table. Spoon the rest of the *pistou* into a bowl for those who would like to help themselves to more. We also usually have a chunk of Parmesan and a small grater to hand so that everyone can also add more cheese if they wish.

TROUT AS A TREAT

"GLORY BE TO GOD FOR DAPPLED THINGS . . .
FOR ROSE-MOLES ALL IN STIPPLE UPON TROUT THAT SWIM."
GERARD MANLEY HOPKINS (1844-1889)

When our children come to beg money for fishing permits, we know for certain that summer's on its way. In France you have to have an official permit for everything – absolutely everything. If your three-year-old daughter wants to dangle a line with a bent pin in the town's river, she has to have a licence. With her photo on it. Just in case some daft fish should by sheer accident collide with her makeshift hook.

More than a few springs ago and with great hopes I bought Daniel his first angling permit – plus a fishing rod, a variety of hooks, sinkers, bait and whatever else was necessary for him to go trout fishing with his friends. I calculated that the outlay would be justified if he brought home even one bunch of trout, because fish, whether freshwater or ocean, is very expensive here. Well, actually, everything is expensive if you come from South Africa, but the cost of fish sometimes still seems to me out of all proportion. We live barely an hour and a half from the Mediterranean and our village is encircled by rivers and lakes alive with fish. But I also know that this is a rapidly diminishing food source – and that a fisherman's life is indeed a hard one.

When we do manage to get hold of fresh ocean fish, they are usually species not found off the South African coast, with names that still baffle me. For instance, the first time that I saw *loup* on a restaurant menu I was quite shocked. Everyone knows that the French eat everything from snails and frogs to horses – but *wolf*? An amused Alain explained that *loup* means not only "wolf" but also a kind of ocean fish, related to the bass. On French menus, as far as he knew, *loup* always referred to the fish and not the canine.

I took this lesson to heart, but I still hardly know one French fish from another. On my weekly trip to market, when I get to the fishmonger's wagon sometimes the only familiar names are sole, which has the same name as in English and *cabillaud*, pronounced almost like South African kabeljou. But the European kabeljou is not the same as the Cape variety that I grew up with. And snoek and yellowtail are of course nowhere to be seen. Then I think, better the devil you know, and opt once again for a few slices of lovely reliable pink salmon, known and adored by everyone at home.

Our other family favourite is trout, by coincidence the first fish that I ever caught myself. Though that catch probably doesn't count because it was on a Boland trout farm where the fish more or less leapt into your hands. Here in France I also helped the children (try) to catch trout and rapidly discovered that in nature it's a lot more difficult than on a fish farm.

That first summer Daniel caught two trout with his new rod – and received one as a present from another angler. After that he got bored, until the next spring, when once again he wanted hooks, sinkers and all the other tackle he had lost in the meantime. (At least it wasn't necessary to buy a new rod.) The second year he once again brought home only three trout – and in subsequent years the catch was sometimes even more modest. Certainly never enough to cover the cost of the permit and the tackle – or even provide a single meal for the whole family.

Now, each spring when I fork out for permits and other necessaries, I no longer dream of the taste of fresh trout with almond flakes, fried in butter. I console myself with the thought that fishing is a healthy outdoor activity for children – certainly much better than violent computer games in a stuffy room – even if no one ever catches a single fish. And if someday someone comes home with a gleaming freckled trout, I will admire its beauty and give poetic thanks for "dappled things". And head at once for the nearest trout farm to buy a few more to feed my family.

Right: Trout in vine leaves

TROUT WITH ALMONDS
SERVES 4

I once ordered this classic French dish in the renowned Le Procope in Paris, one of the oldest restaurants in the world and according to Frommer "the holy grail of Parisian cafes". It was a favourite hangout of Voltaire, Rousseau, Diderot and a long list of other intellectuals down the centuries. Le Procope's trout was too buttery for my taste and in other restaurants it was again too dry. Nowhere was it as delicious as the trout from our Herein River cooked in our own kitchen. Not an objective judgment, granted, but who can be objective about a passion like food?

4 medium-sized trout, cleaned and with heads and tails removed |
200 ml milk | 2 T flour | 1 T oil |
150 g butter | 125 g almond flakes |
2 T parsley, finely chopped | 1 lemon, quartered | salt and pepper

Rinse the fish under cold running water and dry with paper towels. Take two shallow dishes, pour the milk into one and spread the flour in the other. Dip each fish first in the milk and then roll it in the flour, shaking carefully to remove any excess.

Heat the oil and 125 g of the butter in a large, heavy pan. Fry the fish gently for about 5 minutes on each side until cooked and golden brown – taking care that the butter does not catch. Arrange on a serving platter, sprinkle with salt and pepper, cover with foil and keep warm.

In another pan, heat the remaining butter until foaming. Add the almond flakes and fry for about 2 minutes over a medium heat until golden, stirring all the time. Scatter the fish with the almond flakes and pour over the butter from the pan. Serve at once, garnished with parsley and lemon quarters.

TROUT IN VINE LEAVES
SERVES 4

Give your next trout a Greek flavour by wrapping it in vine leaves – like the well known dolmades (balls of savoury rice in vine leaves). If you don't have fresh leaves to hand, you can use tinned ones.

4 medium trout, cleaned |
4 T olive oil | 1 T chervil, chopped |
2 T chives, chopped | 12 large vine leaves, washed and dried |
salt and pepper

Rinse the fish under cold running water and dry with paper towels. Season inside and out with salt and pepper.

Combine half the olive oil in a bowl with the chervil and the chives. Stir until you have a smooth, thick mixture and add a pinch of salt. Use a teaspoon to spread the herbs and oil on the inside and outside of each fish.

Wrap each fish in 3 vine leaves – the head and tail can stick out – and tie with thin twine. Place on oiled paper in a roasting pan and bake for 12-15 minutes in a preheated oven at 210 °C. When cooked, snip the twine and serve at once.

BERRIES AND CHERRIES

"O RUDDIER THAN THE CHERRY, / O SWEETER THAN THE BERRY."

JOHN GAY (1685-1732)

The French call them *fruits rouges* – red fruit – although their colours range from deep pink to purplish black. They include all the soft berries (strawberries, mulberries) and brambles (raspberries, blackberries) that are for me one of the great taste sensations of summer. Not to mention the cherries, especially those juicy black ones they call pigeon hearts. You would have to have a heart of stone not to fall for a fruit with such a poetic name.

But the most romantic berry of all has to be the strawberry – which rather resembles a plump red heart on a Valentine card. For centuries strawberries have been associated with Venus, goddess of love. When two people share a double strawberry they're supposed to fall in love – better remember that when Valentine's Day comes around again. It won't work for us in Europe, because Valentine's Day is celebrated in winter, when strawberries are hard to find.

The honey-sweet Mara des Bois, which was developed two decades ago in southwest France, is today grown all over the world. But strawberries have been prized for centuries by the French – and not only for dessert. In Napoleon's time, the renowned beauty Madame Tallien liked to bathe in the juice of fresh strawberries. Each bath required nearly 50 kilograms of fruit – just as well that the French didn't bath every day then …

As with asparagus, the season of the summer berries is over in a flash. And so we enjoy them, morning, noon and midnight, while we can. The good news is that some berries freeze extremely well and although South Africa, unlike Europe is not blessed with a breathtaking range of red fruits, you can now also buy frozen blueberries, raspberries and other members of the extended berry family.

We prefer not to buy frozen fruit – because it runs counter to our basic food philosophy of the right product in the right season – but when it comes to food there are very few rules that I would carve in stone for posterity. And because brambles grow wild where we live and may be harvested freely, every summer I pick enough to preserve at least part of my harvest in the freezer – together with raspberries and other small berries that make a fleeting appearance at the morning market. Then I can use them later in the year in a tart or as a tasty garnish for a creamy pudding.

And whenever I casually announce that I picked the berries for the dessert myself I notice that everyone at the table seems to tuck in with extra relish. Or perhaps it's just my fertile imagination, because as a former child of the city it is still an incredible delight for me to be able to collect wild fruit and herbs. Also perhaps because this kind of free food is becoming scarcer as the towns spread across the countryside around us.

I would also love to boast about the mushrooms that I gather every autumn, but I have discovered, to my disappointment and shame, that I have no talent for this pastime. Even if I go out with a group of neighbours into the *fôret* and stay within spitting distance of them all the time, at the end they will have collected enough mushrooms for a magnificent meal while I will have found just two, one of which is usually poisonous.

Thank heaven I don't have to search for blackberries, though. Every summer when these little fruits shine so irresistibly in the hedges along my favourite walks, my self-respect is restored as I follow proudly in the footsteps of my hunter-gatherer ancestors. Whenever I go walking or cycling, I take a plastic bag so that I can bring home the little joys along the road. I keep an eye open not only for blackberries but also for wild figs, wild garlic, thyme, dandelion for salad and wild flowers for the table. Sometimes, I must confess, I grab a few pinky-orange apricots or dark red cherries in a neglected orchard. Then the moral line between "collecting wild foods" and "stealing fruit" becomes slightly blurred. But when it looks as though the fruit is only being enjoyed by birds and insects, isn't it a shame to let it simply hang there until it rots?

TARTE AU FROMAGE BLANC
(CHEESECAKE WITH RED FRUITS)
SERVES 8

250 g shortcrust pastry (bought or home-made, see Indispensable on page 179) | 200 g fromage blanc (or smooth cottage cheese) | 3 T pouring cream | 125 g sugar | 3 eggs, separated | finely grated rind of 1 lemon | 75 g fresh or frozen blackberries, raspberries or blueberries (or mixed red fruits) | icing sugar for dusting

Roll out the dough and line a buttered tart pan. Prick the bottom here and there with a fork.

Mix the cottage cheese, cream and sugar in a bowl. Add the egg yolks and lemon rind and stir gently until combined. In another bowl, whip the egg whites until stiff and fold into the cheese mixture.

Spoon the mixture into the pastry shell and sprinkle with 50 g of the red fruit. Bake in a preheated oven at 180 °C for 10 minutes. Reduce the temperature to 150 °C and bake for another 30-40 minutes. Test with a thin knife – the cheesecake is cooked when it comes out clean. Allow to cool before transferring carefully to a large platter. Sift over a thin layer of icing sugar and arrange the remaining red fruits over the tart.

DUCK FOR SALAD

If you should be lucky enough to have some leftover duck meat, you can combine it with one kind of red fruit or a variety – cherries, raspberries, blueberries – to make a quick and delicious light lunch. In France we can buy thin slices of cold duck, *magret de canard*, which is ideal. Lay a bed of corn salad or watercress on a large platter, arrange the red fruits on top, tear or snip the flesh into strips and scatter among the fruit. Scatter with snipped chives and drizzle with a classic French vinaigrette (see page 177). Break off a chunk of baguette to wipe your plate clean.

RED FRUIT SURPRISE
SERVES 4

When you have to make food for children (or, alas, adults) who shy away from leaves, it's safer to stick to convention and serve red fruits as a dessert. But you can always rescue convention from boredom by adding something unusual. Every time I make a good old vinegar pudding for French guests, they are amazed that vinegar can be used in a sweet. South Africans who are familiar with vinegar pudding, will be less surprised to discover what a little vinegar can do for a fruit salad.

500 g mixed red fruits (strawberries, raspberries, stoned cherries, blueberries and more if possible) | 2 T brown sugar | 2 T balsamic vinegar | a few black peppercorns | small mint leaves

If you use frozen fruit make sure it's completely thawed before mixing it with the rest of the ingredients or your salad will be watery. Large strawberries can be cut into smaller slices. Mix the brown sugar with the balsamic vinegar and peppercorns and add to the fruit in a handsome glass bowl, mixing carefully. Remember that red fruits such as raspberries bruise easily. Garnish with mint leaves and leave in the fridge for 15 minutes before serving.

SAVOURING SPINACH
(AND OTHER "FUNNY" VEGETABLES)

"NEVER FORGET TO REPEAT MONSIEUR PRUDHOMME'S FAMOUS REMARK: I DON'T LIKE (SPINACH) AND AM GLAD OF IT, BECAUSE IF I LIKED IT, I WOULD EAT IT – AND I CAN'T STAND IT."

GUSTAVE FLAUBERT (1821-1880)

All too often I am reminded of Monsieur Prudhomme's absurd comment by the steadfast refusal of our children to eat certain vegetables. Sometimes I despair of preparing balanced meals for a whole family when one will not eat aubergine or courgettes, another will not touch peas or tomatoes and a third will eat nothing except peas and tomatoes. But then I remember how deadly boring my own taste was as a child and take heart from the hope that one day they will also realise what they have been missing.

The list of vegetables that I hated (often without even tasting them) was distressingly long. Anything "exotic" (such as asparagus or mushrooms) and anything "green" (avocado pear or cucumber for example) were automatically added to my blacklist. "Orange" vegetables, such as pumpkin and carrots, I ate under protest simply because I was brainwashed into believing they would improve my eyesight and make my hair curl. By my early teens, long straight hair and John Lennon's little round glasses had become the rage and so carrots and pumpkin got the thumbs-down too.

At the same time, in an effort to look as thin and androgynous as possible, I attempted the first of many daft diets – and realised that vegetables may be eaten in great quantities without putting on weight. And this is where the tables began to turn for me. By my eighteenth year I was mad about greens – and not just because most them are a lot less fattening than cheesecake and doughnuts. I had actually begun to enjoy them.

From then on my taste buds became more and more adventurous. When I found myself in France in my late thirties, I was eager to try new tastes and unfamiliar combinations. And my palate was at last mature enough to appreciate everything. As Clifton Fadiman so rightly observes: *"Where is the tongue, the palate that is truly grown-up before thirty? The ability to enjoy eating, like the ability to enjoy any fine art, is not a matter of inborn talent alone, but of training, memory and comparison."*

Nowadays I regularly eat vegetables like endive and bulb fennel, unknown to me as a child. And turnips and leeks, which I had never known how to cook, as well as other greens of which I had never heard until recently. Such as salsify, which is eaten in France even by children. And cardoon (Spanish artichoke) and Jerusalem artichoke, which also bears the delightful French name of *topinambour* – enough to tickle the curiosity of any keen gastronome.

I also realised that what I had always thought of as spinach was actually Swiss chard. It belongs to the same family as the cardoon and has a thick white stem, while spinach in France is a delicate little leaf with a much softer stem. And so I keep learning, every day. I now know that spinach was brought to Spain from Asia by the Arabs, where the learned Ibn al-Awwan described it in the twelfth century as the "captain" of leaf vegetables. The Italians gave the dark green leaves the same imaginative welcome they accorded to numerous other new foods (think of what they achieved with rice, pasta and ice cream), giving it a unique twist by using it for example as a filling for tortellini, ravioli and other kinds of pasta. The Greeks combined spinach with yoghurt, feta and garlic; a few centuries later the Americans made it the staple diet of a cartoon sailor named Popeye – and in our health-conscious age the triumphal progress of Captain Spinach continues.

As a family, we often sit down to delicious, healthy greens such as spinach, artichokes and endive beneath our plane tree. We have even got our children so far as to *like* artichokes and spinach. Endive we're still working on.

By the year 2030, when our youngest turns thirty, hopefully they will all be adult enough to appreciate even endive.

Right: Spanish spinach delight

SPINACH SALAD WITH GOAT'S MILK CHEESE

Fresh raw spinach leaves taste heavenly in a salad with crumbled goat's milk cheese and slices of sweet orange, drizzled with a warm nut and herb dressing. Heat a few tablespoons of olive oil and toss in a finely chopped garlic clove with a handful of chopped walnuts. Stir in the juice of an orange and some chopped watercress leaves (or chives) and a handful of fresh herbs such as parsley, basil, mint or whatever. When the dressing is nice and hot, drizzle it over spinach leaves, cheese and oranges slices, which you have arranged in a shallow bowl. Grind over a few turns of salt and pepper and eat at once.

SPANISH SPINACH DELIGHT

SERVES 4

This dish of Catalan origin we sometimes eat cold as a salad (drizzled with a little balsamic vinegar), but it's also very good hot from the pan, as an accompaniment to fried fish, in an omelette or even as a late breakfast on a lazy weekend morning with scrambled eggs and toast. You can (if you really must) also make it without the garlic.

4-5 T raisins (or sultanas) | 750 g fresh spinach (or Swiss chard), hard parts of the stems removed | 4 T olive oil | 4-5 T pine nuts | 5 fresh garlic cloves, finely chopped | salt and pepper

Place the raisins in a bowl, pour over boiling water and soak for 15 minutes until plumped out. Drain well.

Meanwhile wash the spinach thoroughly under the cold tap. Do not drain, but put straight into a large pot over a gentle heat. Cover with a lid and cook for 5 minutes, stirring occasionally until the spinach wilts. Now drain it in a colander. Press it with the back of a wooden spoon to remove all excess liquid. Chop the spinach coarsely.

Warm the oil in a wok or deep pan over a low heat and roast the pine nuts and garlic until golden brown. Add the raisins and the spinach, raise the heat to medium and stir-fry for 1-2 minutes, until the spinach is hot and all the ingredients are well mixed. Add salt and pepper to taste.

IF LEEKES YOU LIKE

"IF LEEKES YOU LIKE, BUT DO THEIR SMELL DISLIKE, EAT ONYONS, AND YOU SHALL NOT SMELL THE LEEKE; IF YOU OF ONYONS WOULD THE SCENT EXPEL, EAT GARLICKE, THAT SHALL DROWNE THE ONYONS."

DR WILLIAM KITCHINER (1775-1827)

No one can accuse the French of squeamishness when it comes to the smell of certain of their favourite foods. Here I learnt to eat – and enjoy! – cheeses with smells potent enough to use as insecticide. Except that French insects, like French citizens, are clearly undeterred by such lethal aromas.

There is a famous dish of rotten bird meat, of which the highly civilised François Mitterrand, former president of France, was reputedly fond. The *ortolan* is eaten once the flesh is well and truly "ripe" ("ripe" being one of those euphemisms that the Frenchman in my house applies to food which I would simply call "stinking"). To make absolutely certain that you inhale the aroma properly, the dish is eaten in bizarre style, with a large napkin draped over your head, even in chic restaurants. Almost like throwing a towel over your head when you steam your face over a bowl of boiling water. That is perhaps an extreme example of olfactory bravery, but there are many other foods with, shall we say, "suspect" aromas which are eaten here both commonly and continuously. Garlic, obviously, especially in the south where we live. And those very *leekes* and *onyons* to which Kitchiner referred in his popular *Cook's Oracle*.

I find it almost incredible that the real name of this British cook and food writer was in fact Kitchiner – but we know that fact is often stranger than fiction. Kitchiner was a contemporary of Brillat-Savarin, but unlike Brillat-Savarin, who liked to call himself a *médecin-amateur* (amateur doctor) he was a real doctor. An eye specialist, to be precise, as well as an inventor of telescopes, an enthusiastic musician and a renowned gastronome. And unlike most food writers in those days, Kitchiner evidently cooked the food, washed the dishes (!) and performed all the other household tasks which he described – a man to gladden any woman's heart.

I must add in all fairness that my own husband is not at all bad when it comes to washing dishes and all those other "household tasks" inescapably connected with cooking. Early on in our relationship, Alain read the first page of my novel *Entertaining Angels*. There was one paragraph that made a lasting impression: "*Men commit suicide like they cook: dramatically and messily. No doubt because they know they don't have to clean up afterwards. There'll always be some woman to do that.*" From that day he has done his best to prove that "we're not all like that".

Actually, I've never believed that all men are messy cooks. But I don't say that to Alain. He might just give up washing dishes.

We enjoy cooking with *leekes* and *onyons*, or *poireaux* and *oignons*, as they are called here. Before I came to live in France, my leek repertoire was limited to a famous cold soup with a misleading French name, which I refer to elsewhere in this book. Onions I did use – but without knowing what I was doing, according to Alain. Like most of his countrymen he's inclined to be fairly strict about onions. You have white onions and yellow onions and red onions, shallots and spring onions and chives, giant granddaddy onions and tiny dollhouse onions (and more, many more, believe me), and heaven help you if you use the wrong onion in the wrong dish. *Faux pas!*

But how was I supposed to know about shallots? Until just the other day South African recipes drew no distinctions. An onion was a generic, which made your eyes water when you peeled it, amen.

Nowadays I choose my onions with more care, but I still do not care for the aftertaste of raw onion in my mouth – and no Frenchman is going to convince me that it's a pleasant smell. I prefer to listen to Jonathan Swift's sage advice: "*This is every cook's opinion / No savory dish without an onion, / But lest your kissing should be spoiled / Your onions must be fully boiled.*"

TARTE À L'OIGNON
(ONION TART)

SERVES 6-8

This classic French onion tart remains a winner for an economical lunch or a first course for a large meal, or cut into squares for *l'apéro* – the important tradition of snacks and drinks before dinner. If you're making it for *l'apéro*, it's better baked in a rectangular pan.

50 g butter | 500 g white or yellow onions, cut into thin strips/slices | 125 g smoked bacon pieces | 25 g flour | 200 ml milk | 6 T cream | 2 egg yolks | freshly grated nutmeg | 250 g shortcrust pastry, bought or home-made (see Indispensable on page 179) | salt and pepper

Heat the butter in a large pan. Fry the onions briefly over a high heat. Lower the heat and cook gently until the onions begin to turn golden brown. Add the bacon and cook until crisp. Stir in the flour and cook for a minute. Add the milk and cream and cook for 5 minutes, stirring occasionally.

Remove the pan from the heat and add the egg yolks. Sprinkle with salt and pepper, grate over a pinch of nutmeg and set aside to cool.

Roll out the pastry and line a buttered 25 cm tart dish. Prick the base here and there with a fork.

Spoon the onion mixture onto the pastry base. Bake in a preheated oven at 180 °C for approximately 40 minutes until the crust is golden brown and crisp. Serve hot.

ALAIN'S LEEK TART

SERVES 6-8

This variation on the onion tart is one of the most versatile ways to use leeks in summer, because it can be served hot, lukewarm or even cold hours later with a green salad.

2-3 large leeks, sliced | 750 ml chicken stock | 250 g shortcrust pastry, bought or home-made (see Indispensable on page 179) | 3 eggs | 3 T milk | 5 T flour | freshly grated nutmeg | 60 g butter | 2 T crème fraîche | 250 g grated Gruyère cheese (or a similar local cheese) | salt and pepper

Simmer the leeks in the chicken stock for 10 minutes. Remove the pot from the heat, take out half a cup of the hot liquid and set aside before you drain the leeks.

Roll out the pastry, line a buttered 25 cm tart pan and prick the bottom here and there with a fork. Bake in a preheated oven at 180 °C for 10 minutes. Remove but keep the oven hot.

In the meantime combine the eggs, milk and flour in a bowl with 3 T of the chicken stock and grate in a little nutmeg. Melt half the butter in the same pot in which the leeks were cooked. Add the drained leeks and allow to sweat over a low heat until the liquid has completely evaporated.

Add the remaining butter and the egg mixture to the leeks and stir continuously for 7-8 minutes until thickened. Remove from the heat. Add the crème fraîche and half the cheese, and salt and pepper to taste.

Spoon the leek filling into the baked tart shell and sprinkle over the rest of the cheese. Bake for 10 minutes, again at 180 °C, until the crust is golden brown.

Right: Alain's leek tart

EVE'S SECRET

"O EXCELLENT! I LOVE LONG LIFE BETTER THAN FIGS."

WILLIAM SHAKESPEARE (1564-1616)

I can quite accept that our children do not care for cabbage or certain kinds of cheese, but simply cannot fathom why they don't eat figs. For me, a fig that has been slowly sun-ripened to the point where it almost begins to ferment with sweetness is one of those heavenly tastes that make life on earth worth living.

At a tender age I was taught that Adam and Eve in the Garden of Eden covered their nakedness with the mercifully large leaves of the fig tree. This after poor Eve could not contain her longing and tasted the Forbidden Fruit – an apple, according to tradition. But have you ever tried to eat an apple on the sly? It's a crunchy, noisy fruit, not nearly secretive enough to be erotic.

I suspect that it was actually a fig that Eve ate. And I don't blame her. Every time I break open a ripe fig and suck out the sweet pink flesh, I realise that only a child could resist such a deliciously sensual eating experience.

But figs also have their spiritual side. It's no surprise to me that in various cultures, from Africa to the Far East, the fig tree is regarded as the Tree of Life and Knowledge. The Bo Tree under which Buddha sat and meditated is apparently also related to *Ficus caricus* and descendants of this sacred tree may still be visited in Ceylon.

Our garden is, alas, not large enough for a fig tree, but just around the corner is a lane with neglected trees that produce the most delicious purple and green figs every summer. I have to take the garden shears to hack my way through to them and the brambles often scratch my hands till they bleed, but perhaps it's this pinch of pain and suffering that makes these figs and blackberries from our "secret garden" taste sweeter than any other fruit I've known. Every summer my daughter helps me to harvest the figs. She still stops short of actually eating them, not raw anyway, but I have

succeeded in seducing her (and her brothers) with fig jam.

Let me at once make it clear. Fig jam is the only jam I make – and also simply because every summer we have these basketloads of free figs which our children refuse to eat. I am definitely not one of those exemplary women who spend the summer months perspiring in the kitchen, cooking jam and canning fruit for the long winter months ahead. I prefer to eat my fill of fresh fruit in summer, while in winter we feast on jams and bottled fruits made by my exemplary French mother-in-law. Anyway, she's so much better at it than I am, I comfort myself when I feel guilty about lying in the shade with a book rather than slaving over a hot stove.

I have however learnt that figs freeze just as well as blackberries and other soft fruits.

It makes more sense to cook the defrosted figs in early winter, when the kitchen is cooler and the flies have disappeared – for jam or dessert or whatever. As you see, I'm not lazy, not really, just practical. Which is why I'm not going to explain here how to make fig jam. Rather freeze your surplus figs and enjoy the summer.

And if this sounds to you like sacrilege, well, you can always contact my French mother-in-law for her jam recipes. Her name is Francine and she also makes a magnificent terrine of hare. Truly, her price is far above rubies. I have other talents, I hope. And heaps of ideas for dishes that you can make with fresh figs, without raising a single bead of perspiration. Yes, even on the hottest day of the year.

In the end, however, the very best way to enjoy a fresh fig is as follows: find a tree with ripe figs. Reach into it and pick one that feels neither too soft nor too hard, but just right. Break it open, admire the pink inside and bring it to your lips. Eat it, there and then, and think with gratitude of Eve, who was also unable to resist this temptation.

FARCIS DE FIGUE (STUFFED FIGS)

For a simple appetizer you need a dozen fresh (or frozen) figs, strips of good bacon and soft goat's milk cheese. Cut a cross in the top of each fig (make sure that frozen figs are properly thawed first) so that it can be opened into quarters but remains intact at the base. Fill the figs with the goat's milk cheese – you could also use Greek feta or Italian mozzarella instead of French *fromage de chèvre* – and wrap each fig closed with a strip of bacon. Grind over a little salt and pepper. Drizzle with honey and a little olive oil and garnish with sprigs of rosemary. Bake for about 25 minutes in a hot oven.

MARINATED FIGS

With more or less the same ingredients as for stuffed figs you can make a marinated salad which is even easier because it requires no cooking. Cut 12 figs (fresh or completely thawed) into quarters and place in a bowl together with a handful of rosemary leaves. Pour over the juice of a lemon, 3 tablespoons balsamic vinegar and 8 tablespoons olive oil. Add salt and pepper and marinate for an hour. Dish onto a bed of rocket leaves together with chunks of goat's milk cheese. You can add a meaty note with a scattering of shredded smoked ham or *jambon cru*.

CHEAT'S FIG ICE CREAM

Even our children, who ostensibly do not eat raw figs, enjoy this home-made ice cream. You can make your own from scratch – if you know how – or you can cheat like we do and begin by buying a tub of good quality ice cream. Allow the ice cream to become just soft enough to mix – it must not melt – and add small chunks of fresh fig, roughly chopped walnuts, almonds and other nuts, previously roasted until golden brown. Stir well and spoon into a non-stick bread tin or a bowl with an attractive shape, and freeze. Turn out onto a large plate a few minutes before serving. Decorate with a few figs in which you have cut a deep cross and opened out to form four-pointed stars. Sprinkle with more nuts. This dish looks and tastes fantastic.

BAKED FIGS AND NUTS
SERVES 6

Right: Baked figs and nuts

It's hard to believe that a dessert which is so easy to make can taste so delicious …

24 figs, fresh or frozen | 200 g flaked almonds (or walnut pieces) | juice of 2 lemons | 6 T runny honey

Cover the bottom of a shallow oven-proof dish with the figs. Scatter over the almonds. Mix the lemon juice and honey in a jug. Pour half over the figs and almonds until it is all thoroughly moistened.

Bake in a preheated oven at 180 °C for 20 minutes. Pour over more of the lemon sauce if the figs begin to look dry. Served hot or cold, with thick cream, pouring cream or ice cream, it's always a winner.

H SUMMER, SUN AND ... SOUP

"SOUP OF THE EVENING, BEAUTIFUL SOUP!"
LEWIS CARROLL (1832-1898)

Hot weather brings us a happy reminder that our children are, after all, not so uncivilised when it comes to food. Because they are all mad about gazpacho.

For a child of Andalusia this cold vegetable soup would be nothing unusual, but our Franco-Afrikaans brood found it a little exotic at first. It didn't take them long, however, to realise why it's so popular in Spain, where summers can be even warmer than in Provence – and why in many Andalusian houses you will always find a bowl of gazpacho in the fridge in the hottest months. It's as refreshing as a bottle of fizzy cool drink, especially if you add a handful of tinkling ice cubes – but with much more nutritional value. It quenches your thirst and assuages your hunger at the same time and also supplies the salt that your body needs when you're perspiring heavily.

So we have two survival strategies when the *canicule* hits us. This is a heat wave when even at night the temperature is so high that you cannot get enough sleep. In the afternoons we close the shutters so that the grown-ups can enjoy a *sieste* – let mad dogs, Englishmen and children run around outside if they want to – and then, come early evening, we make a huge bowl of gazpacho that can be kept in the fridge for days, as they do in Spain.

The only snag being that our children are now so keen on gazpacho that the bowl is usually empty within a day.

Gazpacho is such a simple, magnificent dish that it always makes me think of Elizabeth David's famous essay "Letting Well Alone", written nearly half a century ago. She recalls how the owner of an inn in a small Provençal town brought her a small bowl of jam as dessert – only jam, without bread or cream or anything else. "*Just jam, and the point about this jam, and I can't help how quaint it sounds, was its absolute rightness.*" The rest of the meal, which included a tomato salad, a home-made pâté, a *gratin de courgette* and a *daube de boeuf* seasoned with fresh thyme and bay leaf, was just as blissfully unpretentious. And then the bowl of jam, home-made naturally – winter melon with a hint of lemon – as the perfect finish.

David continues, in highly entertaining vein, to describe the same meal as it might have been presented in a smart London restaurant. All the unnecessary ingredients, flourishes and garnishes that would have been added – "*a little frill here, a trimming there, an extra vegetable, a few mushrooms in the beef stew ...*" Do read it, or read it again, in the collection *An Omelette and a Glass of Wine*. The title of the book is itself an ode to culinary simplicity.

It's true that London restaurants – and British diners – have become much more sophisticated since Elizabeth David wrote "Letting Well Alone". And it's at least partly owing to this great food lover's hugely influential books and articles. But visitors from elsewhere – and I don't mean just the British – are still sometimes amazed at how simple and yet delicious the food of the French countryside can be, at how simple good food can be, or how good simple food can be.

Under our plane tree we eat very simply on the whole because we can't afford frills – and because those frills take time that we can put to better use. Lying and reading in the hammock under the same tree, for instance, or relaxing with friends around our table, enjoying a glass of cold pink wine from the local cellar. And later when we get hungry, we eat something simple and refreshing, like the summer soups on the next page.

If anyone should ever complain that our food is too plain, I would always be able to quote from *An Omelette and a Glass of Wine*: "*The art, or the discipline, call it which you like, of leaving well alone is a prerequisite of any first-class meal ... So is the capacity, among the customers if you are a restaurateur and among your friends if you are an amateur cook, to appreciate well when it is left alone.*"

GAZPACHO
SERVES 4-6

Right: Gazpacho

2 slices white bread | 3 garlic cloves, finely chopped | 3-5 T olive oil | 500 g tomatoes | 2 cucumbers | 1 onion | 1 green pepper | 2 T good wine vinegar or lemon juice | 500 ml cold water (or tomato juice) | 2 slices brown bread | salt and pepper

Break the white bread into pieces. Mash or blend with the garlic and a pinch of salt. Gradually add a stream of olive oil, stirring continuously until you have a thick, evenly textured paste. Allow to stand for 30 minutes.

Meanwhile peel the tomatoes (plunge them into boiling water first), cucumbers and onion and core the green pepper. Cut half of the vegetables into small cubes and mash the rest with the garlic paste. Dilute with the vinegar and cold water. (Or replace the water and vinegar with tomato juice, which will make an even more delicious soup.) Add the cubed vegetables and chill for at least 2 hours in the fridge so that the flavours can combine and develop.

Cut the brown bread into cubes and fry in the remaining olive oil until crisp, for croutons.

When you are ready to serve the soup, season to taste with salt and pepper and sprinkle with the croutons. We often add a few ice cubes, especially if the soup seems very thick, for an even more refreshing meal.

TOMATO SOUP WITH MARINATED TUNA
SERVES 4-6

This soup is delicious hot or cold. If you omit the tuna, it becomes a tasty fresh tomato soup, always a triumph of summer simplicity.

1 x 500 g fillet of tuna | juice of 1 lemon | 4 T olive oil | 3 shallots, finely chopped | 12 ripe tomatoes, peeled and chopped | 3 garlic cloves, finely chopped | a handful of basil leaves | 200 ml pouring cream (optional) | celery salt, salt and pepper

Cut the tuna into the smallest cubes possible, pour over the lemon juice and leave to marinate in the fridge for at least 15 minutes.

Heat the olive oil and fry the shallots until they are soft and golden. Add the tomatoes, garlic and basil. Stir and season with a pinch of celery salt, salt and pepper. Simmer gently for 10 minutes.

Blitz in a food processor until smooth. Keep hot if you want to eat the soup hot, or leave it for a while in the fridge. Spoon into bowls and add the marinated tuna. If you like, add white swirls with a thin stream of cream, and drop in a basil leaf or two.

Culinaria

European Specialties

Culinaria
KÖNEMANN

KOOK EN GENIET S.J.A.de VILLIERS

Auguste Escoffier

A GUIDE TO MODERN COOKERY

THE ART OF EATING

M.F.K. FISHER

BRACKEN BOOKS

COOKING FROM CAPE TO CAIRO

DORAH SITOLE AND TRUE LOVE MAGAZINE

THE ESSENTIAL COOKBOOK

ASIAN

La cuisine provençale du Mas Tourteron

MACMILLAN

ELIZABETH DAVID

An Omelette and a Glass of Wine

KÖNEMANN

MULTICULTURAL MEALS

"SOMEONE WHO RECEIVES FRIENDS AND GIVES NO PERSONAL CARE TO THE MEAL PREPARED FOR THEM, IS NOT WORTHY OF HAVING FRIENDS."

JEAN ANTHELME BRILLAT-SAVARIN (1755-1826)

From the outside our house looks typically Provençal, with stone walls, blue shutters and a lavender bush at the kitchen window – but inside it's a different story. We are what you might call a multicultural *ménage*. Every day we talk to one another in three languages – and in the kitchen there are cookbooks in more than three languages. Sometimes we eat Provençal food off enamel plates bought at a farmers' co-op in the South African platteland. Or classic French dishes on a tablecloth of shweshwe cotton print from Africa.

When we entertain our friends and family from other countries, we give them typical Provençal or French dishes – that's one of the reasons why they're here, after all. But when we cook for ourselves, or for our French friends, colleagues and acquaintances, we like to be adventurous. "*Melangeons les cultures!*" is a favourite exclamation of Alain's when he gets inspired at the stove or the table, like when we sit down to a typical English breakfast of bacon and eggs and toast and marmalade and he decides that his eggs will taste better with a fat wedge of Camembert …

We enjoy entertaining most when there is a buzz of different languages around our table. Sometimes it sounds like a meeting of the United Nations under the plane tree. For instance, a year or three ago in the summer holidays, a dozen young people came to repair the dilapidated roof of a centuries-old *lavoir* (wash-house) that stood in the vineyards a little way out of town. They slept in the school building and worked every day in the blazing sun. We overheard these international volunteers speaking Japanese and Spanish in the town square; we saw them buying tinned food in the local shop to heat up on a primus stove and we couldn't resist the temptation to invite them over for a decent cooked meal. And at the same time to say thank you for their hard work on the *lavoir*.

That evening we had to carry out extra tables and all the chairs in the house, because in addition to the team of young workers we had our usual quota of summer house guests to feed, including a friend from Montpellier and one of Daniel's mates from elsewhere in France. And then we thought we might as well invite a few other young people like Hakima, who lives around the corner. If you're cooking for twelve, you might as well cook for twenty.

We made a tagine because it's an easy and economical dish – with an exotic feel – more specifically a chicken tagine because other kinds of meat might have religious or health implications for guests whom you don't know. We followed that with a vast green salad of different leaves and fresh herbs from the garden. And lots of long French loaves and a little cheese. All washed down with the red Côtes du Rhône that we tap like petrol out of big tanks into plastic cans at the co-op in the neighbouring town, and then decant into bottles and flagons at home. For dessert we had a few fig tarts made with fruit picked the day before in our *jardin secret* – the overgrown lane with forgotten fig trees, lilacs and brambles that I wrote about in an earlier chapter.

It was the kind of meal I love. Easy, without pretension and with fresh ingredients from our own garden, town, or district wherever possible – and talk in many languages beneath the plane tree until late into the night. It might have gone on even later if our guests had not had to get up at the crack of dawn to work on the *lavoir*. One of the messages they wrote in our informal visitors' book is still one of the loveliest compliments we've ever received from a guest: *Votre maison, votre histoire et votre vie respirent la tolérance et l'ouverture sur le monde.* "Your house, your story and your lives simply breathe tolerance and openness to the world."

I sometimes wonder what has become of Muro from Kyoto, Heang-Mi from Korea, Olga from Spain and all the others. And if they realised that their lively multilingual presence that evening brought us as much pleasure as our simple tagine seemed to bring them.

TAGINE WITH CHICKPEAS
SERVES 4-6

Right: Tagine with chickpeas

Our family's favourite tagine for a weeknight, made with beef frikkadels and chickpeas, is one of those recipes where you can take a short cut or the long way round. The long road is to make the meatballs yourself and soak the dried chickpeas overnight. The short cut (which I usually choose for weeknights) is to use bought meatballs and tinned chickpeas.

300 g or 1 large tin of chickpeas | 6 T olive oil | 2 onions, finely chopped | 4 tomatoes, roughly chopped | 3 large peppers (red, yellow and green), cut into strips | 18 small beef meatballs | fresh coriander leaves | cumin, salt and pepper

If you're using dried chickpeas, soak them overnight in a bowl of water – you can add a tablespoon of baking

HAT TRICK
A tagine is an earthenware container – a shallow dish with a lid that looks like a Basuto hat – in which spicy Moroccan stews are cooked and served. As with the Provençal tian, the name of the container has in time come to refer to the food itself. We usually cook our tagines in an ordinary pot on the stove, but Hakima and other friends of Moroccan origin assure us that any stew will taste even better cooked under this delightful hat of a dish.

soda too – and then simmer over a low heat for about an hour. Tinned chickpeas let you off all this.

Heat half the olive oil in a large saucepan and fry the onions, tomatoes and peppers for 5-10 minutes. Sprinkle with a pinch of cumin and salt and pepper, add the chickpeas, cover and simmer over a low heat for 30 minutes.

Meanwhile heat the rest of the olive oil in a pan and fry the meatballs for a few minutes until golden brown. Spoon the vegetable mixture into a shallow serving dish (or a real Moroccan tagine) and arrange the meatballs around it.

Garnish the tagine with coriander leaves and serve with steaming hot couscous.

ICY ADVENTURES

"MANY YEARS LATER, AS HE FACED THE FIRING SQUAD, COLONEL AURELIANO BUENDIA WAS TO REMEMBER THAT DISTANT AFTERNOON WHEN HIS FATHER TOOK HIM TO DISCOVER ICE."

GABRIEL GARCÍA MÁRQUEZ (1927-)

This, the beginning of Nobel prizewinner Márquez's *One Hundred Years of Solitude*, remains for me one of the best opening sentences of any novel. The reader is immediately confronted with a dramatic situation – a character in mortal danger – and his recollection of a magical moment from childhood.

Ice, and especially that first taste of ice on the tongue, remains an enchanting experience for most of us. As the American writer Heywood Brown put it a century ago: "*I doubt whether the world holds for anyone a more soul-stirring surprise than the first adventure with ice cream.*"

I must however confess that I am not nearly as addicted to ice cream as I am to chocolate. Our children are mad about ice cream – which perhaps explains my preference. Ice cream's milky "childish" taste is like Proust's famous Madeleine cake. It brings back memories and takes you back to happier times, warming your heart (while chilling your mouth), but it's not an "adult" taste like dark or bitter chocolate.

Please note that I'm not talking about real home-made Italian *gelato*. To compare *gelato* with mass-produced factory ice cream is like hanging ultra-fine silk stockings and stretch nylon pantyhose on the same wash line. They're just not in the same class.

But *gelato* is expensive and hard to find where we live and I doubt that our children are able to appreciate the difference. They devour any ice cream too quickly to taste it properly, which is why I don't really bother to make any myself. If I weigh my time and trouble against the few minutes that it would take a swarm of greedy boys to lick the bowl clean, it adds up to a long run for a short slide.

But ice cream without the cream is another story! The Italians conjured up ice cream in the sixteenth century, but they were enjoying sorbet and granita at

least a thousand years before that. Some authorities believe that sorbet, like pasta, was originally brought to Italy from China and the Far East. True or not, the Roman Emperor Nero used fleet-footed slaves to bring snow from the mountains to his kitchens. Here it was mixed with honey, wine and other seasonings and served as an exotic dessert. This new sensation spread quickly through the Empire, most importantly to Sicily, where Mount Etna supplied the ice. Today *granita Siciliana* is still widely regarded as the best granita in the world. After the Mafia, it's probably Palermo's most famous product.

These days a machine-made version of this icy treat is sold everywhere, from French beaches to South African cinemas. It's more refreshing than ice cream because it's closer to a drink, but the slush that you buy in a throwaway plastic cup is only a feeble offshoot of Palermo's granita. Or the magnificent granita that you can make in your own freezer.

On the next page you'll find an explanation of how to make sophisticated granitas in the proper, leisurely way. Or you can choose the short cut and cheat by using your food processor to mix any combination of fresh fruit with a little lemon juice and a few ice cubes. Especially if you want to seduce unwilling children into eating fruit. A fruit ice is cooler – literally and figuratively – than dishing out peaches and plums. If you take this short cut, you don't have to add sugar, because the pulp of the fruit binds the mixture effectively. The texture may not be as crystalline as it should be – but I bet you the kids won't mind, and if it gets really blazing hot, you too won't have the patience to wait four hours for your perfect fruit ice.

So go for the food processor – and stretch out in a hammock with your fake granita. Then read *One Hundred Years of Solitude* again: "*That distant afternoon when his father took him to discover ice …*"

SANGRIA ICE
SERVES 6

40 g sugar | juice of 1 orange (plus a few strips of peel as garnish) | juice of 1 lemon | 500 ml rosé or red wine | 500 ml sparkling wine | 1 green or yellow apple, peeled and sliced | 1 pear or peach, peeled and sliced | a handful of strawberries (or melon cubes or peeled and pitted grapes – or whatever fruit you have to hand) | a pinch of grated nutmeg | a pinch of ground cinnamon

Combine the sugar with 200 ml water in a large pot and heat slowly until dissolved. Bring to the boil and allow to simmer for 3 minutes. Add the orange and lemon juice, the wine and sparkling wine and set aside to cool. Then pour into a glass bowl, add the fruit and spices and chill for at least an hour in the fridge.

Remove the fruit from the syrup with a slotted spoon and keep in the fridge. Pour the syrup into a large, shallow metal dish and place in the freezer for 2 hours. After this follow the instructions alongside for a basic granita – take out every hour, scrape and stir with a fork until no liquid remains.

Divide the fruit among six glasses and spoon the sangria ice over the fruit. Garnish with strips of orange peel. Cheers!

GRANITA NITTY-GRITTY
For a basic granita you need 1 cup of water and half a cup of sugar, 3 cups of fresh fruit juice (preferably from fruit you've pulped and strained yourself) and 2 teaspoons of lemon juice. Combine the sugar and water, bring to the boil and allow to cool to room temperature. Add the fruit juice and pour into a shallow roasting pan or other metal dish no more than 4 cm deep. Remember, the deeper the container, the longer the freezing process will take.

Place in the freezer. Remove the pan after half an hour (make it three-quarters of an hour for a deeper container or a larger quantity) and use a fork to stir the mixture thoroughly. The idea is to break up the frozen parts into small chips, what the French call *paillettes* or sequins of ice – and to mix it all very well with the remaining liquid. Return to the freezer and remove again after half an hour (or three-quarters of an hour, as above) and stir again with a fork. Repeat the process once or twice more until no liquid remains. Just before serving, scratch once more, taking care to retain the crystalline structure.

ADVENTUROUS ICE
Once you've mastered the basic technique – which takes only a little patience and practice – you can experiment to your heart's content. If you add a few tablespoons of vodka for instance, you won't need to stir as often because the mixture will not freeze as hard. (And if you have a few slurps of vodka while you wait, the time will also pass more quickly.) You can also add white wine, dessert wine, even various liqueurs to create seductive fruit ices for adults.

And what about a vegetable ice as a first course? When it's so hot that your guests' appetites are dulled, a granita of cucumber and white wine is an inspired way to begin a meal. Follow the basic granita instructions – and don't forget the lemon juice, otherwise the cucumber will taste too sweet. Instead of fruit juice, use a cup of white or sparkling wine, together with the juice of one or two peeled and seeded cucumbers. Stir only once an hour. Serve this lovely pale green granita in glasses, and decorate with mint leaves. Or coriander leaves, or nasturtium flowers … get creative with granita, and you'll have fun on ice all summer long!

Right: Sangria ice

FAMOUS FRENCH SOUPS

"There are two types of onions, the big white Spanish and the little red Italian. The Spanish has more food value and is therefore chosen to make soup for huntsmen and drunkards, two classes of people who require fast recuperation."

Alexandre Dumas (1802-1870)

After a decade or so in France, I know that there are many more than two kinds of onions, but we still follow Dumas's advice when we make onion soup. We choose the large white onion, because although we are neither hunters nor drunkards, we do know a class of people who require fast recuperation. They are our house guests, who come from far and wide, arriving exhausted by the long journey to our village – and keen to make a quick recovery so that they can explore the beauty of the Provençal landscape.

Of course we know that onion soup is not summer food. It's a dish that tastes best on a winter evening with a glass of red wine in front of a crackling fire. But believe it or not, even in the south of France, the sun doesn't always shine in summer. We have windy days, rainy days, even cold days when the usual summer dishes of salad and *pistou* soup and ratatouille are just not what we need or want. It's then that we find comfort in a bowl of onion soup with a slice of toasted baguette that floats like a little boat and finally sinks beneath its golden cargo of melted cheese ...

Anyway, it would be unthinkable for me not to write about onion soup in this book, because that's how it all began. A few years ago gourmet and publisher Kerneels Breytenbach came to see us on his way back from the frenetic Frankfurt Book Fair. It was obvious that this poor exhausted person needed fast recuperation and so Alain made him some onion soup. Kerneels became delirious with enjoyment – and in fact made such a quick recovery that he was able to feast on numerous other dishes over the next three days.

Because Kerneels had in his day been a restaurant critic for various publications, we decided from the beginning that we would not try to impress him with all kinds of sophisticated dishes that he could eat in any trendy restaurant. We took him to the inn on the corner for a simple country meal. We took him to Chez Claudette in the next village, an unpretentious café with paper tablecloths where jovial truck drivers, local businessmen in neat suits and well-informed tourists in shorts flock at lunchtime for an excellent but affordable four-course meal. And we also fed him our own everyday home-made food.

Kerneels flew back to Cape Town inspired and began to sound me out regarding the possibility of a cookbook. Initially I resisted, but Kerneels persisted and began spreading rumours about Alain's miraculous onion soup. A year or so later Ansie Kamffer, a publisher with the same firm, arrived at our house to continue the campaign, under the plane tree. No, I protested, our food is too simple. That is precisely the point, countered Ansie. Simplicity was what she was looking for. At this a gleam appeared in Alain's eye. He murmured that he wouldn't mind doing the cooking (not at all, never, of course not) if I wouldn't mind doing the writing ...

Well, I couldn't quench that gleam, could I? So I've been writing for months, thanks to a bowl of onion soup.

Bear in mind, this is a dish that can make you cry at least twice. First, when you peel the onions, and then again from sheer bliss when you slurp up the last mouthful. You could also follow the example of hunters and drunkards of note by pouring the remaining red wine in your glass over the last of the soup and bread in your bowl. And then you may weep again, that all good things must come to an end.

WHAT'S IN A NAME?

For a long time I thought that vichyssoise was a French dish because it has a French name – which is about as silly as thinking that my grandmother was French because her maiden name was Du Plessis. For decades there's been a trans-Atlantic tug-of-war over the origin of this great soup.

Most (American) sources say that, on a hot day in 1917, Louis Diat, chef of the Ritz-Carlton in New York, had the bright idea of serving the simple leek and potato soup of his childhood cold. He named the new creation after Vichy, a city not far from his French home town. A quarter of a century later, Vichy became widely known, unfortunately not for its soup but because it was the seat of French government during collaboration with the Nazis in World War II. There are still Frenchmen today who find vichyssoise hard to swallow – simply because of the name.

Other (usually French) sources claim that the chef Jules Gouffé devised the recipe and published it in a cookbook as long ago as 1869. All that Diat did was to serve it cold and give it a name that would look good on the menu of a smart American restaurant: *Crème vichyssoise glacée*. Seeing that Gouffé and Diat were both French, and seeing that the recipe undoubtedly has a French origin, in my modest opinion it remains French – whether it was dreamt up in America or Antarctica.

SOUPE À L'OIGNON
SERVES 4-5

50 g butter | 750 g onions, thinly sliced | 2 t sugar | 2 t flour | 1 litre beef stock | 4-5 thick slices of baguette | 50 g Gruyère cheese, grated (or a similar local cheese) | salt and pepper

Melt the butter in a pot and add the onions and sugar. Cook the onions very slowly over the lowest possible heat for 20-30 minutes, stirring regularly. The onions must become a dark golden brown without burning.

Add the flour and stir-fry for another 5 minutes, still over a very low heat. Add the stock and salt and pepper. Raise the heat and bring to the boil, stirring all the while. Turn down and allow to simmer for 15-20 minutes.

Meanwhile toast the baguette slices. Place a slice in each soup bowl and top with a thick layer of grated cheese. Ladle the hot soup over the bread and cheese. While you eat the soup, the cheese and the softened bread melt – and so will your heart.

VICHYSSOISE
SERVES 4-5

This soup can also be served hot on a cold day, sprinkled with curry powder or scattered with crispy bacon bits, or simply as a traditional French leek and potato soup.

30 g butter | 3 leeks, thinly sliced | 1 onion, finely chopped | 3 medium potatoes, peeled and thinly sliced | 1 litre chicken stock | 250 ml pouring cream | 1-2 T chopped chives | salt and pepper

Melt the butter in a pot and sauté the leeks and onion over a low heat. Stir regularly to prevent them browning.

Add the potatoes and the stock. Bring to the boil, cover and allow to simmer for 15-30 minutes until the vegetables are tender.

Blend the mixture, season with salt and pepper, stir in the cream and allow to cool further. Scatter with the chopped chives just before you carry it to the table.

Right: Vichyssoise

Orange
Légion : le 1er REC défile à Paris

La Provence
HAUT VAUCLUSE

LUNDI 13 JUILLET 2009

FOOTBALL

Adil Rami veut rejoindre l'OM
Le défenseur a décidé de quitter Lille.

Maryse Joissains vire en tête à Aix

Le maire UMP sortant obtient 43,31% des voix, Medvedowsky (PS et Modem) 34,08%. Les Verts (11,31%) se désisteraient pour lui.

Mitterrand fait son festival

Les virus de fièvres estivales étudiés
Une enquête a débuté le 1er juillet à Marseille. Elle porte sur sept pathologies.

Sarkozy se livre sur France 5
Le magazine "A visage découvert" ce soir à 20h35 est consacré au Président.

Nous sommes tous distraits au volant
Une étude livre le Top 20 des sujets de distractions dans les voitures.

TRACS

Alinéa
OUVERTURE

ROLEX
DOUX

e veux
e l'OM

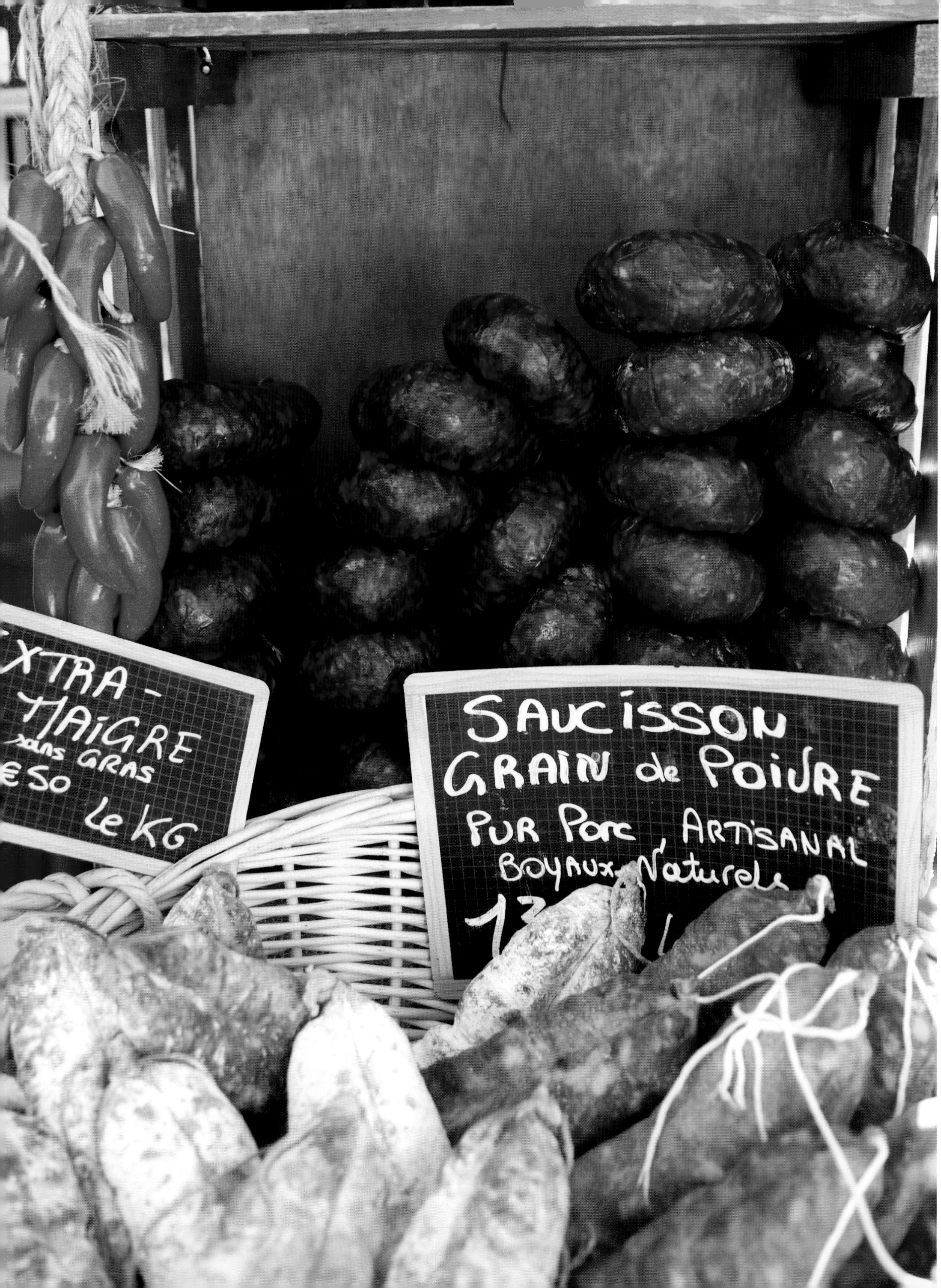

SAUCISSON
GRAIN de POIVRE
PUR PORC ARTISANAL
BOYAUX NATURELS
13

A VERY SPECIAL STEW

"A horse, a horse! My kingdom for a horse!"
William Shakespeare (1564-1616)

Never mind Richard the Third, who was so keen to swap his kingdom for a horse. We have more than once had guests from the Arabian countries of the Middle East who were only too ready to exchange all their earthly possessions for a pig. (Or rather, a tasty piece of pork.)

I had not realised before how many South Africans worked in Saudi Arabia or similar faraway and exotic places where pork is either extremely scarce or banned, on religious grounds. I would also never have described my countrymen as great pork lovers – anyway certainly not equal to the French and other Europeans, who transform pork into the most wonderful pâtés, hams, sausages and other succulent treats.

It's an old truth, however, that anything prohibited immediately becomes more desirable. Just ask anyone who's ever been on a strict diet. You dream about that forbidden slice of bacon, cake or chocolate. You wake up salivating, mad with craving, ready to hand over your children for a single mouthful. Or am I the only one who becomes prey to such wickedness when I try to diet?

Months in advance of their coming, one such group of South Africans from the Arabian countries informed us that they were so starved of bacon and ham, dried sausage and other piggy delights that they were planning a pork tour of France. They wanted to eat as many pork products as possible – and in the process they would also try to discover the perfect cassoulet, the king of all pork dishes. In Toulouse, of course, which is the birthplace of cassoulet, but also elsewhere.

Because there are those who believe that the best nougat does not come necessarily from Montélimar, where it originated, but from Sault, which is much further south. (Do not mention this to anyone from Montélimar.) Or that you will not find the best *salade niçoise* in its *terre natale* of Nice, but in Marseilles or Cannes or Grasse. There are even some who allege that Marseilles is not the best place to eat the renowned *bouillabaisse de Marseille*!

Thus we found ourselves making a majestic cassoulet in the middle of a sweltering Provençal summer. Everyone knows that this is a dish for cold winter nights – but our visitors were desperate and you do not argue with desperate people. And, guess what, we tucked into Alain's cassoulet just as enthusiastically as our starving guests. So the next summer we did it again. Cassoulet is a dish that demands time and effort, better undertaken for a large group of appreciative guests than your ungrateful children, and most of our guests come to visit in summer.

Since that first triumph, it has become a tradition. Every summer, at least once, we prepare the famous stew from Toulouse. French friends are sometimes slightly shocked when they hear about it – but not one of them has ever refused an invitation to come and eat cassoulet under our plane tree on a steamy summer evening. Sometimes the weather even plays along, becoming unexpectedly windy or rainy, driving us indoors to eat. It's the one summer evening when I don't resent bad weather.

To make a proper cassoulet you need three different kinds of pork. Extravagant, I would once have said, before France taught me to appreciate pork. In my previous life I would rather have eaten lamb or beef, but in France I quickly realised that pork is the only red meat that is really affordable. Apart from horsemeat – for which I'm still not ready.

It's a cultural thing, I realised, when for the first time I saw Alain's dear refined sister and her family sitting down to succulent slices of horsemeat. I believe you should try everything once before you die, but I'm quite prepared to die without trying horse, or cat or dog even once. This irrational repugnance has helped me to understand how my Jewish and Moslem friends feel about pork. It's a cultural thing.

I am nevertheless grateful that I don't have to be kosher or halaal. I sometimes wonder how I would have fed my family without the affordability and versatility of French pork.

CASSOULET *TOULOUSAIN*

SERVES 6-8

Right: Cassoulet *Toulousain*

This is not a cheap dish because it requires four kinds of meat – and because *confit d'oie* is traditionally one of the ingredients. But it would definitely be even more expensive if most of the meat were not pork. And if you don't have a goose in the yard that you can quickly slaughter to obtain the pure white, much-prized fat, you can leave out the *confit d'oie*. Even in France it is often listed as optional.

500 g dry white beans | 375 g boned pork belly | 1 ham hock | 2 carrots, thickly sliced | 1 onion, peeled and stuck with 3 cloves | 2 tomatoes, peeled and chopped | 2 garlic cloves, finely crushed

FOR THE SAUTÉ
3 T olive oil | 375 g boned shoulder of lamb, cubed | 2 onions, finely chopped | 2 garlic cloves, finely crushed | 2 tomatoes, peeled and chopped | bouquet garni (see Indispensable on page 177) | 2 Toulouse sausages (or other fat pork sausage), cut into thick slices | 250 g confit d'oie (goose fat – optional) | 75 g dry breadcrumbs | salt and pepper

Soak the beans overnight in cold water. If you're using salt pork belly and ham, you can also soak them to reduce the saltiness. Put the drained beans, pork belly and ham in a large pot together with the carrots, onion, tomatoes and garlic. Add 1½ litres of water and bring to the boil. Cover and allow to simmer for 2 hours until tender.

Meanwhile heat the olive oil in a deep pan and brown the lamb meat lightly on all sides. Add the onions and garlic and continue to sauté until soft and golden.

Scoop enough cooking liquid from the pot with the beans to cover the lamb completely. Add the tomatoes, the bouquet garni and salt and pepper to taste. Cover and allow to simmer gently for 1½ hours.

Brown the sausage quickly in a smaller pan, add to the lamb and simmer for another 10 minutes.

Remove the pork belly and ham from the beans and cut into chunks. Transfer half of the beans to a large ovenproof dish. Place the ham and the pork belly on top, the *confit d'oie*, if you have it, and the lamb and sausage with their cooking liquid. Cover with the remaining beans and finish with the breadcrumbs. Bake in a preheated oven at 150 °C for an hour.

This is a dish which may be eaten without any accompaniments. All you need is a glass of good red wine to lubricate your throat and enough bread to wipe your plate clean.

CHEZ LES CH'TIS

"FRANCE EATS MORE CONSCIOUSLY, MORE INTELLIGENTLY, THAN ANY OTHER NATION ... WHICHEVER FRANCE EATS, SHE DOES IT WITH A PLEASURE, AN OPEN-EYED DELIGHT QUITE FOREIGN TO MOST PEOPLE."

MFK FISHER (1908-1992)

One day, for certain, I am going to undertake a gastronomic treasure hunt through France. In every region, city and town I shall set out to sample that particular culinary product which has made the place well known – and, frequently, world famous. The cheese of Camembert, the melons of Cavaillon, the mustard of Dijon, the sausage of Toulouse …

So I dream sometimes as I sit under the plane tree peeling peaches or slicing beans. Because in this land of gastronomes each *département* and *région* has its own unique delicacies. This is not to imply that I ever grow tired of the sunny olive-oil cuisine of the south. But variety remains the spice of both life and family meals and menus.

I must admit that for me the language, the vocabulary and the accent of each region are almost as fascinating as the food. Here in the south many of our neighbours speak with a Provençal accent. Words are uttered more slowly, and are more drawn out than in, say, Paris. (Thank heaven, because in Paris I might have struggled even more to understand my neighbours.) But the most important characteristic of the local accent is the way in which words that end in -*in*, acquire a lazy nasal resonance. *Vin* (wine) is pronounced *wêng*, *demain* (tomorrow) as *demêng*, and my husband's name as *Alêng*.

Alain came originally from the north, and because his whole extended family still lives in and around Lille, we visit there regularly. And every time as we draw closer to Lille, the strangest thing happens. *Alêng* suddenly becomes *Oleh*. The northern French have a tendency to pronounce "a" as "ô", almost like those born and bred Pretorians who speak *Ofrikôns*. I have often wondered if there might be a connection between round sounds and northerly cities.

The most characteristic sound in the French spoken near the Belgian border is an "s" that becomes "cht". It's the reason why the natives are generally known as Ch'tis. A year or two ago the Ch'ti culture was given a huge boost by a film, *Bienvenue chez les Ch'tis* (Welcome to the Sticks), a comedy that within a few months became the most popular French film ever. Suddenly the whole world wanted to drink Ch'ti beer, eat Ch'ti food, simply be Ch'ti.

Beer, because in the north more beer (and other stronger liquor) is consumed than wine, while the south remains a world of wine (something else it has in common with South Africa). When it comes to Ch'ti food, it's more filling, richer, creamier (note that I avoid the word "unhealthy") than the cuisine of the south. Think of cheeses that stink to high heaven, such as Maroille and Vieux Lille. Think of potatoes and every possible way of cooking them, including the renowned *frites*, which actually originated across the border in Belgium. Think of massive plates loaded with mussels, devoured with those same *frites*. And *potjevlees* or *Flamiche* – Flemish or Dutch names for dishes borrowed from Flemish and Dutch neighbours.

In the lovely city of Lille, the Flemish language is everywhere. In traffic signs, in cuisine, in the surnames of the residents. (It's the only city in France where my surname doesn't meet with a puzzled frown.) And in a restaurant in Lille one chilly evening (all evenings in Lille are chilly if you come from the south) I tasted an unforgettable dessert with the name *Ch'tiramisu*. It's made like a classic Italian tiramisu, but with those delightful Dutch spiced biscuits known as speculaas, which makes a sensational difference, believe me!

Back home in the south *Ch'tiramisu* soon became one of our family's favourite desserts. It's the ideal combination of all our different cultures – the Ch'ti roots of Alain and his sons and the Dutch antecedents of me and my children – plus a Mediterranean-Italian origin that suits our sunny environment. But let me be honest. Even without those clever excuses we would have been mad about it.

CH'TIRAMISU
SERVES 6

200 ml cream | 5 T sugar | 4 egg yolks | 500 g mascarpone cheese | 200 g speculaas biscuits | 4 T strong black coffee | cocoa powder

Whip the cream with a tablespoon of sugar until stiff. In another bowl, use the highest speed of an electric beater to combine the egg yolks with the rest of the sugar until thick and creamy. Gradually add the mascarpone and then the whipped cream, still using the electric beater, but at a lower speed.

Line a shallow dish with a layer of biscuits. Moisten with a little of the coffee – just enough to make the biscuits damp, not soft. Cover with a layer of the cream mixture. Add another layer of biscuits and moisten again with coffee. Cover with a final layer of cream and sprinkle with cocoa powder. Refrigerate for at least an hour before serving.

CHEAT'S TIRAMISU
SERVES 4

I have called this one cheat's tiramisu because it requires far less beating than a "real" tiramisu. The secret of its special flavour is the combination of honey and cinnamon.

½ t ground cinnamon | 4 T strong black coffee | 300 g mascarpone cheese | 4 T runny honey | 200 g sponge fingers | 250 ml cream | 30 g caster sugar | cocoa powder

Mix the cinnamon with the coffee and pour over the mascarpone. Add the honey and beat until smooth.

Break the sponge fingers into pieces and arrange a layer in each of four glasses. Add a layer of the mascarpone mixture, then another layer of biscuits topped with a layer of mascarpone, until the glasses are almost full.

Whip the cream until stiff, add the sugar and divide among the four glasses. Use a tea strainer to sprinkle a little cocoa powder over the cream in each glass. This dessert may be eaten immediately but it's just as delicious if you leave it in the fridge for later.

Right: Cheat's tiramisu

TIMELY AND UNTIMELY TARTS

"THE WORLD BELONGS TO THOSE WHO
DON'T HAVE A FIXED HOUR FOR MEALS."
ANNE JULES DE NOAILLES (1650-1708)

It took me a long time to come to grips with the traditional formality of the French apéritif. Where I grew up we also like a drink before dinner, but it's an informal affair where you improvise as you go along. Usually, as soon as a guest walks in the door, a drink is thrust into his hand. It's part of our famous South African hospitality, isn't it? Sometimes a bowl of peanuts might be balanced on the arm of a chair, or a plate of cheese nibbles plonked on a coffee table; at other times you might forget completely about the snacks and your guests won't even notice. They are there for a meal, after all, not for crisps and peanuts.

In France it works completely differently. L'apéro is a complicated ritual of mysterious rules and unwritten commandments – and woe on you, stranger in Jerusalem, if you don't have some grasp of the basic principles. Strangely enough too, here in the sunny south these rules are even more strictly applied than in the chilly north where Alain grew up.

I was scarcely a week in Provence, still unpacking my suitcases, when a neighbour invited me over for my first official apéro. Thank you, I'd love to come, I responded in my broken French, what time should I be there? Bof, Sylvie murmured with that famous French shrug, l'heure de l'apéro. "The hour of the apéritif." An answer both unhelpful and absurd – obviously the hour of apéritif is the time to drink an apéritif, but this is the reply I still get, more than a decade later, when I'm invited for l'apéro.

Meanwhile I have managed to learn that the l'heure de l'apéro means not too long before dinner, but also not too close to dishing up either. Enough time therefore, to relax and drink a glass or two and eat a snack or two – because l'apéro without anything to eat is as unthinkable as a Provençal summer without lavender – but not enough time to get tipsy or spoil your appetite for the actual meal. We're talking now of dinner – but even here you can't be sure, because on weekends and holidays an apéritif may be served before lunch. And precisely *when* dinner will be served can vary according to the season, the weather and the inclination of the hostess.

All very confusing for someone who has not grown up in the tradition of l'apéro. And frustrating because if you arrive too early, you must sit and wait with parched throat for the other guests before you get a drop to drink. But to arrive too late is perhaps even worse. Then the other guests may be fed up with *you* because they've had a long and thirsty wait. One of the unspoken rules here where I live is that everyone must be present before the apéritif begins officially. There are however some charitable hosts who will offer you a drop en attendant ("while you wait").

But once the guests have all arrived the refreshments usually more than make up for the wait. The selection might include olives stuffed with sweet peppers, dried sausage filled with nuts, little slices of bread spread with black or green tapenade, pheasant pâté and celery sticks and other savouries so seductive that you can get completely carried away. And spoil your dinner – which would be a great shame, because a hostess who lays on a good apéro, will ten to one also serve an outstanding meal.

That's why I favour the increasing popularity of l'apéro allongé – an extended apéritif served instead of the usual four-course meal. I also find it an attractive option if I'm the hostess. Many of the classics of a Provençal apéro like the olives, the aubergine caviar or the dried sausage you can simply buy at the market in the morning. Then in the late afternoon you can bake an easy tomato tart or a pissaladière, which is all you need to impress your guests. Cut it into squares so that they can eat with their fingers. Much less trouble than a proper meal – and much less washing up.

But if I ask people over for an apéritif, I always give them a time. I don't think I shall ever be French enough simply to murmur a vague "à l'heure de l'apéro…"

PISSALADIÈRE
(PROVENÇAL ONION AND ANCHOVY TART)

SERVES 6-8

DOUGH
25 g yeast | 375 g flour | 50 g soft butter | 2 eggs, beaten | pinch of salt

FILLING
6 T olive oil | 1 kg onions, thinly sliced | 12 anchovy fillets | 50 g black olives | freshly ground black pepper

Dissolve the yeast in 4 tablespoons lukewarm water. Sift the flour and salt in a large mixing bowl. Rub in the butter with your fingers. Make a hollow in the middle of the flour and pour in the beaten eggs and dissolved yeast. Mix with the flour until you have a soft dough.

Place the dough on a floured surface and knead until smooth and elastic. Roll into a ball, cover with a damp cloth and leave in a warm place for 30-45 minutes until risen and doubled in size.

Meanwhile heat 4 tablespoons of the oil and fry the onions over a low heat for about 20 minutes until golden. Stir now and then to prevent the onions catching.

Knead the risen dough for a few minutes and roll out into a circle of about 25 cm. Place it on a greased pizza pan or a flat baking sheet.

Spread it with the onions. Arrange the anchovies in a latticework over the onions and garnish with olives (which you can halve and stone, if you're feeling energetic). Season with a grinding of pepper and drizzle over the last of the olive oil. Leave in a warm place for 15 minutes to rise again. Bake in a preheated oven at 230 °C for 15-25 minutes.

EASY TOMATO TART
SERVES 6-8

I had always felt that savoury tarts spelt trouble – or at least a lot of bother for an uncertain outcome – until I discovered the easiest tomato tart in the world. The children call it a pizza tart because it's very flat and very good – as good as pizza. The other similarity to a pizza is that you can give your imagination free rein with whatever you pile on the basic dough.

If we want to whip up a quick snack we line a flan tin with a roll of bought puff pastry, spread it with pesto or *pistou* or black or green tapenade or even aubergine caviar – in fact any Mediterranean-type spread we have to hand. Then we add a good layer of grated cheese – Parmesan, Gruyère, or a mixture of leftover cheeses from the fridge – and then cover the cheese with thin slices of tomato, overlapping them like fish scales. Or, if we happen to have cherry tomatoes, we cut them in half and lay them down cheek to cheek, cut side down. It all adds up to a tart as pretty as a picture, one that needs no other decoration. Just before the tart goes in the oven, give the tomatoes a nice sheen with a thin drizzle of olive oil. If you've used tomato slices you can add more grated cheese or slices of mozzarella, or black olives or even pieces of *jambon cru* or smoked ham. Bake the tart in a preheated oven at 180 °C for 20 minutes. Cut into large slices or small squares.

IS *PISSALADIÈRE* PIZZA?
Pissaladière is often described as a traditional Provençal pizza, related to the "white pizza" of the Italian Liguria region which is made without tomatoes or cheese. Other sources declare that it has nothing to do with a pizza – except for a totally coincidental similarity in the name. *Pissaladière*, they say, is derived from *pissala*, a fish paste made long ago on the Provençal coast between Marseille and Nice. The granddaddy of the present day *pissaladière* was covered with this fish paste – later replaced by anchovies – and could be bought from bakeries early in the morning for breakfast. Almost like English anchovy toast!

Right: Easy tomato tart

OSTRICH WITH FRENCH FLAIR

"ALL PARADISE OPENS! LET ME DIE EATING
ORTOLANS TO THE SOUND OF SOFT MUSIC!"
BENJAMIN DISRAELI (1804-1881)

Once a year – and usually only once a year – I cook unadulterated *boerekos*. Around Freedom Day, April 27, which coincidentally also falls close to my birthday, a longing comes over me to cook a Sunday lunch exactly like my mother used to make, for a table packed with guests. *Slaphakskeentjies* (traditional cooked onion salad) and saucy bean salad and chicken pie and bobotie and yellow rice studded with raisins. Renée from Rochegude brings a milk tart or three, I ask another expat to bring along biltong or *blatjang*, I take down a jar of my father's green fig preserve from the shelf – and we feast for the fatherland.

We always invite a mix of French-Afrikaans couples and expats from elsewhere – Italians, English, Dutch, Americans. Sometimes there may be even one or two bona fide citizens of France without any South African or international connections.

This is about the only major meal of the year when Alain steps down as executive chef and I take charge of the kitchen. He helps to peel the onions for *slaphakskeentjies*, shreds chicken for the pie and performs other lowly tasks usually allotted to me. For this event I am the Big Kahuna. It could not be otherwise. Alain cannot even pronounce a name like *slaphakskeentjies*, let alone prepare it.

For the rest of the year we combine French, South African and all kinds of dishes without any purist pangs of conscience. Alain calls it *rapprochement des cultures*, which according to him has to begin in the kitchen. And Elmarie and Stephan are two of our guests who certainly agree. Elmarie is yet another Afrikaans girl who was led astray by a Frenchman and his food. (They have an Afrikaans-French daughter who is a little younger than our Mia – a striking example of cultural rapprochement.) Elmarie was a waitress at a London restaurant where Stephan worked as a chef, which is how they met. They now cook for a living and have opened a small restaurant, L'Esclafidou, in the historic heart of Nîmes, where they make entrancing French dishes with a *boerekos* twist. Or South African staples to which they bring a refreshing French flair. Such as a compote of figs and rooibos tea, served with slices of grilled fish, or an exceptional interpretation of a Malay lamb curry, or the most delicious morsels of bobotie in a crisp crust of *millefeuille* …

Some of Stephan's more sophisticated dishes we wouldn't attempt ourselves – why be satisfied with a copy when we can enjoy the original in their restaurant, served by the charming Elmarie? I did however beg the recipe for one of his creations that is simple enough to attempt in our own kitchen. It's an ostrich dish which will bring you out in goosebumps of pleasure. And no, you don't eat it with a napkin draped over your head, as with the much prized *ortolan* that I have written about in another chapter – although such a gesture would not be out of place with the ostrich's legendary habit of hiding his head while leaving the rest of his body exposed. You may however, like Disraeli, be moved to exclaim: "*All Paradise opens!*"

Imagine then, a sosatie of succulent ostrich fillet on a bed of couscous laced with a Mediterranean marmalade of sweet pepper, the whole anointed with rocket pesto oil. That's culinary cross-pollination for you! The soft music playing in the background can vary from Brel to the Briels, from Sanseverino to Miriam Makeba. Anything, absolutely anything, is possible when you begin to cross cultures …

Right: Ostrich sosaties with couscous marmalade

OSTRICH SOSATIES WITH COUSCOUS MARMALADE
SERVES 6

COUSCOUS *EN MARMELADE*
300 g couscous (semolina) | 100 ml olive oil | 50 g softened butter | 1 sweet red pepper, thinly sliced | 1 green pepper, thinly sliced | 2 large onions, thinly sliced | 1-2 garlic cloves, finely chopped | 1 branch of thyme | 1 bay leaf | 100 ml red wine vinegar | 1 can (about 400 ml) chopped tomatoes | salt and pepper

ROCKET PESTO OIL
100 g rocket | 20 g pine nuts | 2 garlic cloves | 300 ml olive oil | salt and pepper

SOSATIES
1,2 kg ostrich fillet, cubed | 1 sweet red pepper, cut into short, broad strips | 1 green pepper, cut into short, broad strips | 1 red onion, cut into broad strips | olive oil

Prepare the couscous with 350 ml boiling water, 1 tablespoon of the olive oil and a pinch of salt. Mix well, cover with clingfilm and leave to stand for 5 minutes. Add the butter and fluff with a fork to separate the grains.

For the marmalade, heat the remaining olive oil and cook the sweet peppers and onions for 3 minutes on high. Add the garlic, thyme leaves, bay leaf and vinegar and cook until most of the liquid has evaporated. Add the tomatoes, season with salt and pepper, turn down the heat and simmer until the mixture acquires a jam-like consistency.

For the pesto oil, combine all the ingredients in a food processor until you have a smooth sauce.

Moisten the cubes of ostrich meat with a little olive oil and seal in a pan until lightly browned. Thread the meat on sosatie sticks, alternating with the pepper and onion strips. Brush with olive oil, season with salt and pepper and slide them under a hot grill, until the meat is cooked to your liking but the vegetables are still crisp.

To serve, mix the couscous with the sweet pepper marmalade and spoon into the middle of each plate. Place a sosatie on top and drizzle a thin stream of pesto around the edge of the plate. Garnish with a few rocket leaves and serve immediately.

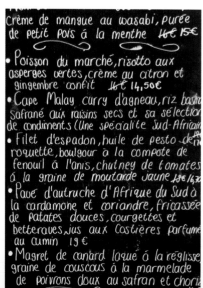

SAY CHEESE

Say what you like about the French, but it's a fact that they can make magic with cheese. Cheese from cow's milk, goat's milk, sheep's milk. Soft cheese, hard cheese, "fresh" cheese, blue cheese, cheese with a waxy rind, cheese with a rind of ash, cheese wrapped in dried chestnut leaves and tied with raffia …

In France, they say, you can eat a different cheese on every day of the year. And even once you get to know the hundreds of different kinds, the variations could keep you busy for many more years. Because two cheese makers living two kilometres apart, both making Picodon (a little wheel of goat's milk cheese for which our neighbouring town Valreas is known), will each produce his own unique version.

Picodon is one of more than forty French cheeses which carry the AOC label. This stands for *Appellation d'Origine Contrôlée*, a guarantee that a product has been made at a specific place using a specific technique, which is also found on the best wines as well as other foodstuffs. There must, I suppose, be some French people who do not like cheese, but I have certainly never met any. In fact, "French cheese lover" sounds to me like tautology, like "retreat backwards". Each French citizen has a favourite cheese, which can usually be linked to the region where he was born or the place where he lives. If you thought South African rugby fans were provincially biased, you should hear a table of Frenchmen arguing about cheese …

Because we're a multicultural family, we're less provincial about our cheese. My daughter likes a soft Tartare cheese mixed with garlic and fresh herbs, perhaps because she was born in Provence; but she's ready to try any cheese, no matter how smelly, blue, old or soft it might be. My son, who was born in Cape Town, still prefers sweeter, more "innocent" cheeses that remind him of the Gouda of his toddler days, like Tome des Pyrénées, which has a black rind and a soft, pale yellow interior. Thomas and Hugo, both born in Lille, like the more robust, "riper" cheeses of the north, like Maroilles or Mun-

ster. Alain is the blue cheese fan of the family. Any one, like Bleu d'Auvergne or Fourme d'Ambert, will gladden his heart but the emperor of blue, Roquefort, can make him sing for joy.

Roquefort is one of those French cheeses like Camembert and Brie, familiar worldwide and imitated everywhere – but millions of people who have tasted Roquefort, are not aware that it is the one blue cheese made from sheep's milk. French children learn these things from infancy; every time they go shopping with *maman*, while they sit drooling among the food in the grocery trolley. In any supermarket the cheese is set out exactly like the meat, categorised according to the animal of origin. Beef, lamb, pork for meat. Cow, sheep, goat for cheese.

If our family had to choose one favourite everyday cheese, it would probably be the Basque sheep's milk cheese Ossau-Iraty. Simple enough for Daniel's stubbornly South African tongue, flavoursome enough for Alain's finicky French taste buds, and fine for the rest of us. But for special occasions like Christmas we choose a special cow's milk cheese sold only in winter, as rich and creamy as a pudding, with the enticing name of Mont d'Or ("hill of gold").

This is a cheese with a downy pinkish skin like a peach, smelling of rich soil, mushrooms and pine forests and melting in the mouth like ice cream – a delight for every sense. Picture putting a bowl of the best ice cream in the middle of the table and giving each guest a spoon to eat straight from the dish. That's how we eat Mont d'Or, from the round spruce box in which it is sold, with spoons to scrape out the last delicious dregs.

In French restaurants you are often presented with a choice between cheese or a sweet as dessert. Initially I could not understand how anyone could choose cheese rather than a tempting *crème brûlée* or a decadent *mousse au chocolat*. Now I know that a cheese like Mont d'Or is as irresistible as the most irresistible chocolate confection. And that, for a chocolate addict, must rank as a major discovery.

FENNEL SALAD WITH BLUE CHEESE
SERVES 4

1 lemon | 3 fennel bulbs | 150 g blue cheese | 150 ml pouring cream | 50 g hazelnuts (or walnuts), finely chopped | freshly ground black pepper

Peel the lemon with a potato peeler or a small knife and set aside a few thin strips for decoration.

Cut the fennel bulbs into thin slices, sprinkle with the lemon juice and steam for 5 minutes.

Crumble the blue cheese into a bowl and grind over the pepper. Add the cream and mix well.

Arrange the fennel slices on a large plate. Sprinkle with the finely chopped nuts and strips of lemon peel. Pour over the blue cheese dressing and serve at once.

ROQUEFORT MARBLE SPREAD
SERVES 4 OR MORE

200 g Roquefort (or a local blue cheese) | 2 T crème fraîche | 100 g fromage blanc (or smooth cottage cheese) | a few raisins | freshly ground black pepper

Mash the Roquefort with a fork. Add the crème fraîche, cottage cheese, raisins and pepper. Mix well, transfer to a serving bowl and cover with clingfilm. Leave in the fridge for a while so that the flavours can develop. Spread on slices of whole-wheat bread. Admire the lovely marble pattern for a few seconds before it disappears into your mouth.

Right: Roquefort marble spread

ARTICHOKES WITH GOAT'S MILK CHEESE
Our local little Picodon cheeses taste delectable baked on artichoke bottoms. (You can replace the Picodon with thick round slices of a local goat's milk cheese.) For each person at the table cook one artichoke and cut off the leafy top half. Then put a Picodon on each artichoke bottom and bake for 4-5 minutes in a preheated oven at 210 °C. Place a little pile of *mesclun* or mixed young salad leaves on each plate, drizzle with French vinaigrette (see page 177), top with the hot artichoke with its melted cheese – and eat at once.

MAD ABOUT "MAD APPLES"

"I DOUBT THAT THE IMAGINATION CAN BE SUPPRESSED. IF YOU TRULY ERADICATED IT IN A CHILD, HE WOULD GROW UP TO BE AN EGGPLANT."

URSULA K LE GUIN (1929-)

If I had to be a vegetable, I wouldn't mind being an eggplant. With her smooth, glossy purple skin and her seductive French name Mademoiselle Aubergine is perhaps the *femme fatale* of the vegetable kingdom – and what woman doesn't sometimes dream of being dangerously irresistible?

The eggplant's origin is Oriental and mysterious – perhaps Indian, perhaps Chinese. All that we know today is that her ancestors were brought to Spain by the Moors in the eighth century. And, like any woman with a shady past, she has connections that are not to be trifled with. She is related to the deadly nightshade family, which includes her notorious cousin belladonna, and it was this connection that inspired some of her most unflattering names, such as "mad apple".

Until the seventeenth century Europeans believed that she could cause fever, epilepsy and madness – but still welcomed her in their gardens because she was so lovely to look at.

In the hedonistic France of Louis the Sixteenth her dangerous reputation seemed only to make her more desirable and she at last took her place at the country's most elegant tables. As might be expected, famous French painters like Cézanne and Matisse found her irresistible and used her as a model. You have only to think of Henri Matisse's *L'intérieur aux aubergines* (1911), with three dark purple eggfruit displayed like precious Fabergé eggs against a flaming orange backdrop.

I salute you, Mademoiselle Aubergine. Greta Garbo and Sharon Stone and other *femmes fatales* of the silver screen could learn a few lessons from you.

On a more pragmatic level, I am grateful that the eggplant is so widely used in Mediterranean and Provençal cooking. Incidentally the name eggfruit (or eggplant) is not as inexplicable as it sounds. We use it as a vegetable, but botanists regard it as fruit, a berry to be precise. And although the large, plump purple variety is today the most familiar to most of us, the aubergine is still grown in various forms all around the world, including small, egg-shaped and yellow or white ones – hence the egg in eggplant. And of course there is also brinjal, the Indian name, which is used in countries where Indian cooking has had an influence.

Here in the south of France, one of the simplest, most delicious things that we do with aubergines is to make them into a purée with the very smart name of *caviar d'aubergine*. For a long time I thought that this "caviar" must either be impossibly expensive to buy or impossibly difficult to make. I was delighted to discover – yet again – that thinking doesn't make it so. Now I make aubergine caviar all the time, to make up for all the years that, through sheer ignorance, I had to manage without it.

Once you've made your eggplant caviar, you can quickly attain the next level of aubergine joy. Use the caviar to make an aubergine loaf, eat it with a purée of fresh tomatoes and a few basil leaves and you will taste sunshine and summer and blue skies, even if it's raining outside. And while your tongue is being treated to the creamy texture of the baked eggplant you'll begin to understand why there is a popular Arab dish with the poetic name of *Imam Bayeldi*. It can be translated as "the imam fainted" – and the swoon of the legendary imam was apparently caused by the incredible deliciousness of this dish made with eggplant.

That kind of gastronomic ecstasy upstages even the French and what MFK Fisher described as their "open-eyed delight" when it comes to eating.

CAVIAR D'AUBERGINE
SERVES 4 (MAKES ABOUT 400 G)

*2 large aubergines | 1 large tomato |
1 garlic clove, finely chopped
| 4-5 T olive oil | 1 T snipped basil
(or parsley, coriander or other fresh
leafy herbs of your choice) | salt and
pepper*

Place the aubergines on the open
rack of a preheated oven and bake at
200 °C for 45-60 minutes, until the
skin becomes slack and the inside is
thoroughly soft.

Meanwhile skin the tomato (plunge
it into boiling water first) and cut
into dice.

Peel the baked aubergines. Keep
half the skin and blend it with the
flesh and tomato in a food processor. (The skin gives the caviar a better texture.)

Fry the garlic quickly in a little oil.
Add it to the aubergine mixture.
Season with salt and pepper. Add
the olive oil in a thin stream, stirring
continuously to achieve a smooth
paste.

Spoon into a bowl, cover with clingfilm and chill for at least 15 minutes in the fridge. Garnish with the
snipped basil when you serve it. It
can be spread on slices of baguette,
or you can dip sticks of carrot or
celery into it, or you can use it to fill
small hollowed out tomatoes … use
your imagination and enjoy.

PAIN D'AUBERGINE
SERVES 6-8

If you want to bake your loaf with
the least possible trouble, you can
buy the aubergine caviar in a jar
or ask someone to bring you a
jar from France. Otherwise make
the caviar according to the recipe
alongside.

*6 eggs | 400 g aubergine caviar |
3 T crème fraîche | salt*

Beat the eggs with the aubergine
caviar. Add a pinch of salt and stir
in the crème fraîche. Spoon the
mixture into a greased loaf tin and
place the tin into a wider, shallow
dish of water (*bain-marie*). Bake
in a preheated oven at 180 °C for
about an hour.

The loaf can be eaten hot or cold.
Cut into slices, garnish with basil
leaves and serve with a *coulis de
tomates* (see Indispensable on
page 179).

Right: Caviar d'aubergine

ARLATEN

Attention ! Musée bientôt fermé !

Fermeture pour rénovation du Museon Arlaten

Dimanche 25 octobre 2009 au soir

CONSEIL GENERAL
cg13.fr

Retrouvez-nous sur
www.museonarlaten.fr

Marseille
Provence
de la culture
2013

STIRRING RISOTTO

*"A DIET THAT CONSISTS PREDOMINANTLY OF RICE LEADS TO
THE USE OF OPIUM, JUST AS A DIET THAT CONSISTS PREDOMINANTLY
OF POTATOES LEADS TO THE USE OF LIQUOR."*
FRIEDRICH NIETZSCHE (1844-1900)

In our house we're partial to rice; we probably eat more rice than potatoes, but in spite of Nietzsche, we continue to prefer alcohol to opium. We like every kind of rice available, from the perfumed basmati of India and the jasmine rice of Thailand to the creamy arborio and carnaroli of Italy, from the wild brown rice of North America to the Calasparra Bomba that our Spanish neighbours use for their famous paella. And naturally we favour the local products of the French Camargue, especially the nutty red rice that has won international renown.

Rice was being harvested in India thousands of years before Christ and still plays an important role in Hindu ritual. In Rajasthan, for example, when a bride enters her new husband's house for the first time she scatters rice everywhere to ensure fertility, prosperity and happiness. In the south of India raw rice is dyed red and thrown over bridal couples – which is probably where our Western custom of bombarding newlyweds with rice, rose petals and confetti originated.

In Indonesia and other countries Mother Rice is also honoured as a symbol of fertility and throughout the East rice has for centuries been an indispensable part of cuisine. Without rice, declares an old Chinese saying, even the cleverest housewife cannot cook. In Chinese the same word is used for both food and rice, so the saying could also be translated as: without food no one can cook.

In Japan little girls are encouraged (threatened is perhaps a better word) to eat up their rice with the warning that every grain a girl leaves in her bowl will become a pockmark on the face of her future husband!

With all these colourful Oriental customs and superstitions around rice, we sometimes forget the wonderful rice grown in the West. Once again it was the Italians who took the lead: just as they seized on pasta (and possibly also ice cream) from the East and made it their own, they have also given rice a unique local character. Today Italy is Europe's largest producer of rice, in particular those firm round-grained varieties that make the most delicious risotto.

Risotto has become popular in South Africa only fairly recently, but has quickly achieved status as a staple for busy cooks looking for easy, delicious and economical ways to feed their loved ones (and who isn't these days?). True, it takes more time than pasta, which you can simply toss into a pot of boiling water – because you must stand patiently stirring at the stove – but the response at the table and the clean plates at the end of the meal will more than reward you for your trouble.

No one can stop you from making your risotto with "ordinary" long grain rice, but you will miss the full, creamy flavour of the round Italian grain. The Rolls-Royce of round grains is the magnificent carnaroli, but if you can't find – or can't afford – a Rolls, then aim for an Alfa Romeo like arborio, baldo or roma. If that's still not within your means – and I understand because my means are also sometimes rather mean – you can always opt for a reliable Fiat like vialone nano or ribe. They may not be *superfino* quality, but are nevertheless good enough for a tasty risotto.

MFK Fisher once observed that for many women cooking is simply a necessity rather than a calling. They are not drawn to the kitchen by the inner voice of an Escoffier, but rather driven there by the rumbling of empty stomachs from husband and children. *"They cook doggedly, desperately, more often than not with a cumulative if uninspired skill."* On days when my own cooking tends to subside into dogged desperation, I take out the rice and a wooden spoon and quietly begin stirring a risotto that I know will make all the faces around our table shine. Risotto, like so many other bright Italian ideas, can save the day for many a weary woman.

MILANESE RISOTTO
SERVES 6

Right: Milanese risotto

There are innumerable recipes for risotto, but I still prefer this classic Milanese version. Risotto originated in that region and the recipe is without complications, simple and full of flavour.

1¼ litres chicken stock | ¼ t (1 g) saffron threads | 2 large beef bones with plenty of marrow (ask your butcher) | 80 g butter | 1 T finely chopped onion | 400 g round-grain rice | 200 ml dry white wine | 100 g Parmesan cheese, grated

Heat the chicken stock. Soak the saffron in 2 tablespoons of the hot stock. Remove the marrow from the bones and allow it to melt together with about 60 g butter in a large saucepan over a low heat. Add the onion and fry gently. Then add the rice and cook until transparent, stirring constantly. Add the wine. Once the rice has absorbed the wine completely, begin adding the hot stock, half a cup at a time. Wait until the liquid has been absorbed before adding more – and keep stirring.

After about 10 minutes, add the 2 tablespoons of stock with the saffron. After 16-20 minutes, the rice should be *al dente* and nearly all the liquid absorbed. Remove from the heat and stir in the rest of the butter and half the Parmesan. Sprinkle over the rest of the cheese and serve at once.

A RISOTTO FOR SPRING

We call this spring risotto because we make it with fresh asparagus, which are only available then. Cut off the tips of about 200 g asparagus and set aside; chop the stems finely. Also finely chop 5 spring onions and 2 cloves of garlic. Heat olive oil in a large saucepan and fry 200 g chopped pancetta (or ordinary bacon) until crisp. Add the spring onions, garlic and chopped asparagus stems and sauté for a few minutes over a low heat. Add 400 g round-grain rice and cook until it becomes transparent, stirring constantly. Pour in 200 ml dry white wine and keep stirring until it is absorbed. Now begin adding 1½ litres of hot chicken stock, half a cup at a time, stirring continuously. When the rice is cooked and the liquid absorbed, remove the saucepan from the heat and stir in 100 g grated Parmesan. Season with freshly ground black pepper. Steam the asparagus tips for 4 minutes. Arrange on the rice together with a few Parmesan shavings and serve immediately.

PURE PEAR PLEASURE

"THERE ARE ONLY TEN MINUTES IN THE LIFE
OF A PEAR WHEN IT IS PERFECT TO EAT."
RALPH WALDO EMERSON (1803-1882)

In early autumn, when it's still warm enough to eat outside, but many of the summer fruits are no longer available, we turn with gratitude to the unassuming pear.

Old English wisdom says that you cannot compare apples and pears – but it's almost impossible not to. Both are ancient fruits that were eaten by our prehistoric ancestors. There are more references to apples than to pears in Greek mythology – just think of the golden apples that Hercules had to find and the apple of discord that ultimately led to the fall of Troy – and yet it was the pear that Homer described as "a gift of the gods".

My personal preference is also for the pear, even if it is only because of François Pierre de la Varenne (1618-1678) and his poetic declaration: "*The pear is the grandfather of the apple, its poor relation, a fallen aristocrat … which once, in our humid land, lived lonely and lordly.*" No, De la Varenne was not a poet, but the very first great French food writer and author of the *Le cuisinier françois* (sic), regarded as the foundation of modern French cuisine. Perhaps in his heart he really was a poet, like so many food writers after him.

The French Comice pear, greeny-yellow and blushing on the outside, indescribably sweet and juicy within, is regarded as one of the best pears in the world. But pears, perhaps more than most other kinds of fruit, must be eaten perfectly ripe. An unripe pear is hard and unpalatable, an overripe one mushy and unpleasant.

To reach perfection, a pear must ripen on the tree, not in the fruit bowl on your kitchen table. Seeing that most of us do not have pear orchards, it's all too easy for us to miss those ten minutes of perfection to which Emerson refers.

Happily there are many plans for the pears that become available in early autumn in an almost-but-not-quite state of perfection. Pears make outstanding partners for other flavours such as red wine, dark chocolate and cheese. In fact, pears and cheese are made for each other. Especially blue cheese such as Roquefort or Bleu d'Auvergne, but also other characterful cheeses such as ripe Gorgonzola or matured Parmigiano Reggiano.

Brillat-Savarin probably spoke on behalf of all Frenchmen when he compared dessert without cheese to a pretty woman with only one eye. My husband certainly shares this view. Nearly every meal in our house is rounded off with cheese. A large meal with cheese and a sweet – first the cheese, then the sweet, because in France the order is important – and a lighter meal with cheese or a sweet. Another enduringly popular option is cheese with a salad.

The cheese and salad possibilities at the end of a French meal are legion. You can serve an ordinary green salad dressed with vinaigrette in a glass bowl and three or four different cheeses on a board and allow each guest to help himself to salad and the cheese of his choice. Or you can present each guest with a plate with a few crisp lettuce leaves and a wedge of cheese – this may sound Spartan, but it's the kind of simplicity that looks and tastes good, provided the cheese is of the highest quality. Or you can place a few rounds of fresh goat's milk cheese on a bed of salad leaves and send it round the table …

Or you might be more original and create your own salad of leaves and cheese. This is where that trusty combination of pear and blue cheese always proves a triumph. Or, if you really must finish on a sweet note (as is often the case with us, because we have sweet-toothed children) then you might serve some blue cheese first and then a few pears encased in shells of dark chocolate for a modern version of the classic *Poires Belle Hélène*. It will make you look with new appreciation upon this "fallen aristocrat" among fruits.

CHICORY SALAD WITH PEAR AND BLUE CHEESE
SERVES 4-6

2 large ripe pears | 1 T lemon juice | 1 orange, peeled and divided into segments | 2 large heads of chicory | 175 g Roquefort (or other blue cheese) | 2 T chopped chives

VINAIGRETTE
3 T walnut oil | 2 T white wine vinegar | ½ t finely grated orange rind | pinch of sugar | salt and pepper

Peel and core the pears, cut them into thin slices and place in a bowl with the lemon juice. Mix well to prevent the slices going brown. Arrange the slices with the orange segments and chicory leaves on a large plate.

Make the vinaigrette by placing all the ingredients in a glass jar, closing the lid and shaking until well mixed. Pour over the salad.

Just before serving, crumble the cheese over the salad and sprinkle with the chives.

Right: Chicory salad with pear and blue cheese

BEAUTIFUL HELEN'S PEARS
Our summer version of the classic *Poires Belle Hélène* is actually a combination of two favourite pear desserts. First we stew the pears in red wine until they turn an exquisite plum colour and acquire a subtle wine flavour. (A pear simply poached in sugar syrup has a childish sweetness which doesn't do it for us.) For 4 large pears, 1½ cups of decent red wine is usually enough. Place the pears (peeled but whole and with the stem intact) in a deep saucepan. Add the wine, 4-5 tablespoons of sugar, the same of lemon juice and the finely grated peel of a lemon. Cover and simmer over a low heat for about 20 minutes or until tender.

Remove the pears and continue to cook the remaining liquid until only half a cup remains. Pour this thick syrup over the fruit and allow to cool. Melt 150g good dark chocolate in a glass bowl over a saucepan of simmering water (*bain-marie*) and plunge each pear into the chocolate until completely covered (this is where the stems come in handy). Place the pears in the fridge so that the chocolate forms a hard shell around the butter-soft red-stained pears – a fantastic combination of colour, texture and flavour.

O-PEAR-A
Poires Belle Hélène (poached pears with hot chocolate sauce served with ice cream) was named after Jacques Offenbach's popular satirical opera, *La Belle Hélène*, first performed in 1864 in Paris. The Helen concerned was of course the beauty who brought about the Trojan War. An apple dessert would have been more appropriate, since the myth actually started with the golden apple promised to Paris if he could choose the most beautiful of three goddesses.

CHIC AS CHICORY

"THE GREATEST SERVICE WHICH CAN BE RENDERED
ANY COUNTRY IS TO ADD A USEFUL PLANT TO ITS CULTURE."
THOMAS JEFFERSON (1743-1826)

The French call this versatile vegetable endive. The English call it chicory and sometimes also French endive. But the French actually stole it from the Belgians, just as they did those famous *frites* that are now known all over the world as French fries.

And if President Jefferson (himself a keen vegetable grower) is to be believed, the French owe their Belgian neighbours a great debt, because chicory is indeed an exceptionally useful plant.

In our kitchen it's an absolute stalwart in winter, when many of our favourite vegetables are hard to find, but because it's cultivated in greenhouses all year round, we also use it in other seasons. I find its subtly bitter taste indispensable in some of my favourite summer salads. Like chocolate, salad often needs a *soupçon* of bitterness to give it a kick.

The ancient Greeks and Romans were familiar with wild chicory and the Egyptians grew it 5 000 years ago as a medicinal plant. The poet Horace described his simple diet as: *"Me pascunt olivae, me cichorea, me malvae."* Olives, chicory and mallow were, it seems, all he needed to sustain him. I can understand the olives and the chicory, but I'm curious about the mallow …

Chicory still grows wild along the roads of Europe, known by the charming name of "blue sailor", because of its violet-blue flowers and also, less attractively, as "coffee weed". The latter name, of course, because for centuries the roots have been dried, roasted and ground as a substitute for coffee.

Like many of my compatriots I grew up with chicory coffee – South Africa and France happen to be the two countries which produce the most chicory – but had never tasted endive. As a leaf vegetable, for most South Africans chicory was as exotic as artichokes.

These days, like artichokes, it is more readily available, but many people sadly still have no idea of how to cook it properly – or how delicious it tastes raw in salads.

Chicory was first exported from Belgium in the nineteenth century, via France to the rest of the world. Legend has it that a Flemish farmer returned to his fields after a long absence and found to his surprise that the roots of his chicory plants had developed white leaves. According to other more reliable sources, the vegetable was discovered in the Brussels Botanic Garden – but just as coincidentally. The gardener was not looking for a new kind of vegetable but simply trying to grow a few familiar greens in a cellar during the winter. He covered the chicory with a layer of loose soil and found that the roots produced delicate white leaves. Hence the Flemish name *witloof* – which simply means "white leaves".

It's the lack of light that keeps the leaves white, as with white asparagus which grow underground – and the whiter the better, because then the leaves are less bitter. That's why endive is often found wrapped in blue paper in the shops to protect the leaves from light and to retain the delicate balance of just a little bitterness in the taste. At the market of Sainte Cecile les Vignes, where I usually buy my vegetables, it's luckily not hidden under any sort of paper. The creamy white leaves with their faint greeny-yellow sheen, make a beautiful picture among the gleaming red of tomatoes, peppers and radishes in summer and the deep greens of broccoli, corn salad and Spanish artichoke in winter. Truly a delight for the eye (and the taste buds, of course) in all seasons.

Last but not least – according to another legend, the blue chicory flower has the magical power to unlock any door. I have not yet tried it because in our safe little village locking doors has not so far been necessary. But it might be a tip worth remembering, if ever you should lose your front door key.

CHICORY SALAD WITH PARMESAN AND GARLIC DRESSING

SERVES 4

3 thick slices white bread, crusts removed | 2 T olive oil | 25 g butter | 4 heads chicory | 50 g Parmesan cheese | salt and pepper

GARLIC DRESSING
3 T natural yoghurt | 2 T mayonnaise (bought or home-made, see Indispensable on page 179) | 1 T finely chopped parsley | 1 clove garlic, finely crushed | 2 T grated Parmesan cheese

Combine all the ingredients for the dressing in a bowl. Add a little water, just enough to make the dressing easier to pour. Season to taste with salt and pepper.

Cut the bread into small cubes for croutons. Heat the oil and butter in a pan and fry the bread for 3-4 minutes, stirringly continuously until the cubes are crisp and golden. Drain on a paper towel and sprinkle with salt.

Arrange the chicory leaves on a large plate and pour the dressing over the lower half of the leaves, where it will collect in the hollows which form natural "spoons". Pile the croutons into the same hollows and shave a few curls of Parmesan over the salad just before serving.

BRAISED CHICORY
There are many ways to cook chicory, but the secret is always to remove the heart, otherwise it will taste too bitter. Simply cut off the base of the leaves and you will see a small dark section on the inside which you can remove with a sharp knife.

We like to braise chicory or to "sweat" it, as Alain says. After you've removed the heart, cut the remaining leaves in half lengthwise. Chop a small onion finely, heat a little oil in a pot and gently fry the onion until transparent. Add the chicory and cook until golden, stirring now and then. Add the juice of half a lemon, a cup of chicken stock, a pinch of sugar and snipped herbs of your choice, such as parsley and thyme. Keep stirring until the chicory begins to brown.

Cover the pot. Turn the heat down as low as possible, and allow to sweat for 15-20 minutes, until no liquid remains. Lift the lid now and then and stir if necessary. Season with salt and pepper and serve as a tasty accompaniment to any kind of meat.

Right: Chicory salad with Parmesan and garlic dressing

GOOD, BETTER, BASQUE

"THE FRENCH ARE WISER THAN THEY SEEM,
AND THE SPANIARDS SEEM WISER THAN THEY ARE."

FRANCIS BACON (1561-1626)

When I read English essayist Francis Bacon's judgment (certainly contentious) on the French and the Spanish, I wonder what to think of the Basques. The Basque culture extends across the border between France and Spain and the bearers of this culture are French and Spanish. Does this mean they are both cleverer than and not as clever as they look?

On the other hand, the terrorist group ETA claim that they are neither French nor Spanish and insist that they must have their own independent state; the Basque language is indeed incomprehensible and, like Hungarian, unrelated to anything else in Europe. I cannot claim to be an expert on Basque politics, but I have had a soft spot for their food ever since I worked in that region as a very young au pair. Basque cuisine, any Basque will tell you proudly, is older than both French and Spanish cuisine.

And better, many will add, just to be provocative.

I wouldn't go so far – especially not in front of my French husband – but it is a robust, flavoursome cuisine that makes liberal use of sweet pepper and chilli, herbs, tomatoes and red sauces. "Sexy" is the word that unexpectedly comes to mind. And if you're wondering how food can be sexy, well then, you've obviously never eaten with lust and total abandon. Who knows, the *poulet basquaise* over the page may just be the beginning of a great adventure for you.

It was not only the food that made a great impression on me during the few months I spent looking after that dark-eyed baby in a small coastal town near Biarritz. It was the way the people ate. And I don't mean only the Basques themselves, but all the French who were spending the summer holidays there. In front of every house stood a table, on a stoep or a balcony or in the garden where families sat and ate with obvious enjoyment at lunchtime and evening all summer long.

For me it was a revelation.

I had grown up in a land of endless sunshine, but I never realised that, weather permitting, you can eat outside *every day*. At a table! Not just next to a braaivleis fire with a paper plate balanced uncomfortably on your lap. Not just when you're picnicking, sitting flat on the ground with plastic glasses that tend to tip over all the time. As a child, if I did sit outdoors at a table, it was usually thanks to the famous local tradition of padkos – a frikkadel and a rock hard egg swallowed at a cement table under a blue gum tree next to a busy national road.

That was more or less my total experience of "eating outdoors".

As a student I sometimes saw Italian and French art films and marvelled at how the people on screen were always gathered around long tables outdoors, feasting. Without ever being plagued by insects or getting sunstroke. In Europe the sun was surely less dangerous and the insects less of a nuisance, I thought. Now that I have lived for more than a decade in the south of France, I know that the sun can be merciless and the flies can be a revolting plague. But that doesn't stop me from eating outdoors as often as possible. After all, there are trees and umbrellas to protect you from the sun and flypapers and other ways of getting rid of bothersome insects.

Because an outdoor meal, with your bum on a comfy chair and your elbows on a sturdy table, is an enjoyable, companionable, sensual affair that can go on for hours, flies or no flies – just as in those art films that I saw so long ago. It's a lesson I learnt in the French *Pays Basque*. That – and how sexy a chicken can taste if you cook it as they do.

POULET BASQUAISE
SERVES 4

4 T olive oil | 175 g smoked ham or bacon, cut into chunks | 4 large portions of chicken | 4 onions, sliced | 3 garlic cloves, finely chopped | 2 green peppers, cored and cut into chunks | fresh marjoram leaves (or thyme) | 425 g fresh (skinned) or tinned tomatoes | 300 ml chicken stock | fresh parsley, chopped | salt and pepper

Heat the oil in a heavy-based pan. Fry the ham over a low heat, stirring until it begins to brown. Remove with a slotted spoon and keep warm.

Place the chicken pieces in the pot and cook, turning occasionally until golden brown on all sides. Remove with a slotted spoon and keep warm.

Fry the onions and garlic in the same pan until soft and golden. Add the peppers and a handful of marjoram leaves and cook gently for 10 minutes. Add the tomatoes and the chicken stock. (If you're using tinned tomatoes in juice, 150 ml stock should be enough.) Season with salt and pepper. Return the chicken and the ham to the pot, cover and cook gently for about 40 minutes, until the chicken is cooked and tender.

Remove the chicken portions and arrange in a shallow dish. Cook the sauce until it is nice and thick. Pour over the chicken, sprinkle with parsley and serve with rice from the Camargue (or good local rice). Like most French dishes with lots of sauce, it's good to have a baguette or two to hand so that everyone can break off a piece to wipe their plates clean.

EUSKADI TA ASKATASUNA
ETA stands for *Euskadi Ta Askatasuna* – "Basque homeland and freedom" – a good example of how strange the Basque language can sound to a European ear.

Right: Poulet Basquaise

ABSOLUTELY FABULOUS FRUIT

"I LOVE FRUIT, WHEN IT IS EXPENSIVE."
SIR ARTHUR PINERO (1855-1934)

We who have grown up in the sunny Southern Hemisphere seldom place a proper value on fresh fruit. Perhaps this is because our best fruit is often exported – to northern countries where people pay highly for their appreciation – or perhaps it's just another case of familiarity breeding contempt. We know nothing of the long white winters of the north when you yearn with your heart, your belly, and your mouth for the first strawberries of spring ...

One of the many things that amazed me when I came to live in France was the ecstasy with which both young and old devoured fresh fruit. In summer a magnificent meal may be concluded with nothing more than a colourful assembly of fruit and the children will fall upon this simple and healthy dessert as greedily as the adults. The fruit is obviously perfectly ripe and beautifully presented, on a bed of shiny leaves, or surrounded by crushed ice, or cut into neat chunks to create a rainbow of colour on a silver platter.

"*The French genius for presentation*" is, according to Elizabeth David, one of the main reasons for the respect which French cuisine continues to command in the rest of the world. Even in the markets of Provence – perhaps particularly in the markets of Provence – this talent is evident. "*Why does a barrow boy selling bunched radishes and salad greens ... know by instinct so to arrange his produce that he has created a little spectacle as fresh and as gay as a Dufy painting?*"

There are also occasions when just one kind of fresh fruit falls straight from the tree to the table as it were, unpeeled, uncut, unvarnished, without even a bowl of caster sugar or a dash of alcohol to anoint it. Shortly before Christmas last year we dined with a neighbour who, at the end of an extended meal, simply placed a bowl of clementines on the table. I was almost tempted to feel indignant – that's not pudding! Yes, after more than a decade here, I am sometimes still too blasé to appreciate fresh fruit. But then I saw with what pleasure the other guests began passing the bowl around. These naartjie-like little oranges from Spain taste their very best at Christmas, when fresh fruit becomes scarce, and the moment the first guest slipped a segment in his mouth, his blissful smile made it clear that this dessert was a winner. And then I noticed that some of the fruit in the bowl had stems, each with a single dark green leaf. I gazed in admiration at the beauty of the leaves against the gleaming orange of the skin. And I realised that this utter simplicity was also a striking manifestation of "*the French genius for presentation*".

By the time the bowl reached me, my mouth was literally watering. I now know that those mandarin oranges were perfect for the occasion – the right fruit in the right season – and that any creamy or more indulgent dessert would have left us oversated.

In summer fresh fruit is even more of a mercy at the end of a large meal. When the heat is quite enough to make you feel uncomfortable, you certainly don't want to be left unable to rise from your chair from overeating. Fruit of good quality, presented attractively and simply as a first course or a dessert will gratify even the most decadent gourmand. And if you don't believe me, I can quote two supreme authorities. A century ago, in his classic *Guide to Modern Cookery* Auguste Escoffier described how to serve fresh figs: "*Place them on a layer of very green leaves, and surround them with broken ice.*" That's all.

And three decades ago Elizabeth David wrote this about fresh mulberries: "*Arrange them in a little pyramid, if possible on shiny green leaves, on a plain glass compote dish, with a separate bowl of sugar.*"

With fresh fruit, elegant simplicity remains the best strategy.

FRESH FRUIT SKEWERS
SERVES 6 (12 SKEWERS)

Right: Fresh fruit skewers

The fruits in this recipe are simply suggestions. In early summer you can make the skewers with red fruits, melon and watermelon, and in late summer with apricots, peaches, plums, pears and apples. Or, in South Africa, with banana, pineapple, pawpaw, guava and mango. Kiwi fruit is always a good choice because of its luscious green colour. Whatever fruit you use, aim for a variety of colours so that your skewers look like bright, chunky beads. Or why not choose only shades of red? Remember the prettier the skewers, the keener everyone will be to try them, even those of us who still do not value fresh fruit as much as we should.

*¼ watermelon | ¼ melon | 3 peaches |
2 bananas | 3 kiwi fruit | 12 strawberries |
12 raspberries | caster sugar*

Peel and pip the watermelon, melon and peaches. Cut into chunks so that you have at least 12 of each kind of fruit. Peel the bananas and cut each into 12 fat slices. Peel the kiwi fruit, cut in half lengthwise, remove the white core and cut into fat slices. Hull the strawberries.

Thread the fruit on 12 wooden skewers. Sprinkle with caster sugar and arrange on a large platter. Cover with foil (light can discolour the fruit) and place in the fridge for a while so that the fruit will be deliciously cool when served.

RASPBERRIES AND FRESH CREAM
Of all the hundreds of ways to enjoy fresh fruit and cream, Raspberries Romanoff is still the very best, according to MFK Fisher. Whip 1½ cups of cream until stiff, gradually adding ¼ cup of caster sugar and ¼ cup Kirsch. Mix the cream with as many chilled raspberries as you like and serve ice cold in tall glasses.

STRAWBERRY SURPRISE
Choose a firm ripe melon and make a cut around the stem end to form a lid. Remove the pips and hollow the centre out with a soup spoon. Sprinkle with caster sugar. Soak a good helping of strawberries in Kirsch (or a liqueur of your choice) and fill the melon hollow with these strawberries and chunks of the melon flesh which you removed. Replace the lid on the melon and chill for two hours in the fridge. Serve cold and watch the delighted smiles of your guests when they discover the contents of this delectable surprise package.

GRAPE SOUP AS A STARTER
Why not begin a summer meal with fruit? On a sizzling hot day, nothing could be better than grape soup. All you need for four people is 1 kg black grapes and 2 tablespoons of snipped coriander leaves. Peel 100 g grapes and keep these aside for decoration. Liquidise the rest in a food processor and strain the juice to remove all skin and pips. Simmer the juice gently for half an hour and allow to cool. Keep in the fridge until just before serving. Spoon into bowls, add the peeled grapes and scatter with the coriander leaves.

PLANS WITH POLENTA

"NOTHING WOULD BE MORE TIRESOME THAN EATING AND DRINKING IF GOD HAD NOT MADE THEM A PLEASURE AS WELL AS A NECESSITY."

VOLTAIRE (1694-1778)

One of the marvels of modern cuisine is that delicacies once reserved for gods and kings, such as asparagus and chocolate, may now be enjoyed by everyone. An even greater wonder, I often think, is that previously poor man's foods, such as polenta, have become the gastronome's delight.

Polenta is the third sacred P in the Italian culinary trinity – Pasta, Pizza and Polenta – which has conquered the world with its unique combination of flavour, simplicity and versatility. At the southern tip of Africa, polenta is not as yet as popular as the first two, and therefore a more original dish to serve guests. But it also comes as a familiar taste to the South African palate, being in fact nothing more than a kind of mealie meal, for which our resourceful Italians have devised some exceedingly clever plans.

The word "polenta" is derived from the Latin *pulmentum*, which centuries ago was the staple food of Roman soldiers and poor peasants. This was a porridge originally made from simple grains such as buckwheat, millet and spelt, but when Columbus returned from the New World with the infinitely superior mealie, maize meal began to replace other kinds of flour. In the northern regions of Italy, maize grew exceptionally well and polenta became more popular than bread. During the food shortages of World War II, polenta saved many an Italian family from starvation.

Somewhere in polenta's long history, someone discovered that, like pasta, it tasted even better with Parmesan cheese. Or with fresh fish, as the Venetians still like to eat it. Or cut into squares and fried in butter and tossed into a green salad for a quick and easy lunchtime snack.

Polenta, like its Arabian cousin couscous/*kuskus*, can be prepared in the traditional time-consuming way or bought as an instant grain in a packet. Purists shudder at the idea of polenta-in-a-packet, but if you grew up with an Italian grandmother who cooked her mealie meal in a giant copper pot over an open fire, stirring it constantly with a huge wooden spoon, you will know that it is hard, hard work. And if you had no such stirring grandmother, you won't know what "real" polenta tastes like anyway. And that's my excuse for buying instant polenta.

In summer, when friends from abroad undertake their annual pilgrimage to our Mediterranean climate, we don't want to waste unnecessary time slaving over a hot stove. We would much rather relax with these pilgrims who bring news and cheer from afar – the Hoogenbooms from New York, the Beyers family from Cambridge, the Younges from Cape Town. With friends like these, we have survived adventures like canoeing down the white waters of the Ardèche, but our greatest adventures are usually gastronomic in nature.

A simple river bank picnic with baguettes of coarse ground flour and demi-salted Normandy butter. A royal couscous lunch for a dozen guests under our plane tree, or a *confit de canard* with butterbeans around our dining table on a windy night with a sickle moon. An *apéro allongé* with homemade aubergine caviar in a flowery courtyard at Hugo and Edith's holiday house, and a sublime polenta with Mediterranean vegetables and a *tarte tatin* on the roof terrace of Glenda and Gavin's holiday home, with a summer thunderstorm threatening to explode over our heads.

That day I realised once again that if you are really enjoying what you eat, then thunder, lightning and even rain will hold no fear for you. We simply moved the table a little further under the overhang of the roof and carried on feasting on Glenda's polenta. By the time we had finished the cheese course and were ready for the *tarte tatin*, the sun was shining again. But even without the sunshine, it would have been a meal to remember through the long, quiet winter months, until the visitors from abroad begin to turn up with the swallows again.

POLENTA *SUD*
SERVES 6

You can prepare the vegetables and pesto for this recipe in larger quantities and store them in the fridge for a few days to use in other dishes like salad and pasta. If you're entertaining, the whole polenta dish can be made a few hours before the meal – ideal if you prefer to relax with your guests instead of slaving over a hot stove while everyone else has a good time.

1 cup instant polenta | a pinch of saffron (powder) | 1 T butter | 3 T grated Parmesan cheese | 6 tomatoes | 3 yellow peppers | 3 red peppers | 3 aubergines | olive oil | flour | basil leaves | salt, coarse salt and freshly ground pepper

PESTO
Make the pesto according to the recipe on page 177.

Make the polenta. Boil 2½ cups of water in a saucepan with a pinch of salt, add the polenta and saffron and stir rapidly to remove all lumps. Keep stirring until the polenta is cooked (about 5 minutes), add the butter and Parmesan and stir again. When the polenta has the consistency of thick porridge, pour it into a greased round or rectangular baking tray. Choose one large enough to ensure that the polenta base is no thicker than 2cm. Leave to set.

Peel the tomatoes (plunge them into boiling water first), cut into quarters and remove the seeds. Place on a baking sheet, sprinkle with coarse salt, pepper and olive oil and bake in a preheated oven at 160 °C for about 25 minutes.

Cut the yellow and red peppers into quarters, removing the seeds, and arrange on a baking sheet with the skin side up. Sprinkle with coarse salt and olive oil. Place under a hot grill until the skins begin to blister and blacken. Remove from the oven and place in a plastic bag to sweat for 10 minutes. The skins may then be easily removed. Cut into slices.

Peel the aubergines, slice lengthwise, place in a colander and sprinkle with salt. Allow to stand for half an hour and then dry with a paper towel. Roll each slice in a little seasoned flour and fry in olive oil in a large pan until tender. Slide the polenta under a hot grill for a few minutes to crisp the surface. Spread with a layer of pesto. Arrange a layer of aubergine slices on the pesto, then a layer of tomatoes, and top with the red and yellow peppers. Season to taste with salt and pepper. Garnish with basil leaves and serve at room temperature.

POLENTA KEBABS WITH GARLIC GREENS
Garlic works brilliantly with polenta and you can make the most delicious polenta kebabs with vegetables that have been marinated in olive oil and garlic. Cook the polenta as described above, allow to set and cut into cubes.

For 8 kebabs, cut 4 courgettes into slices, 250 g broccoli into large florets and 1 sweet red pepper into fat strips. (Or dream up your own combinations of veggies.) The broccoli (or other vegetables) can be blanched quickly in boiling water, though we prefer to eat it as raw and crisp as possible. Mix the veggies in a bowl with 2 finely crushed garlic cloves, olive oil, salt and pepper. Allow to stand for half an hour so that the vegetables are well flavoured by the garlic.

Thread the vegetables and polenta cubes alternately onto kebab sticks. Grill for 7-8 minutes under a hot grill, turning frequently. Remove from the oven, sprinkle with grated Parmesan cheese and eat while still hot.

Right: Polenta *Sud*

A MAN LOVES MEAT

"DOTH NOT THE APPETITE ALTER? A MAN LOVES
THE MEAT IN HIS YOUTH THAT HE CANNOT ENDURE IN HIS AGE."
WILLIAM SHAKESPEARE (1564-1616)

Theo is another South African who has lived in the south of France for much longer than I have. Like many South African men, he is a great rugby enthusiast. He also enjoys cooking and entertaining friends. It was probably inevitable that our first meal together would be scheduled around a Springbok rugby test.

That day the food had to be swiftly prepared, before the TV broadcast of the test began, so Theo made a fire outside and, while we enjoyed an *apéro* on the patio, he quickly seared a few slices of fresh tuna on the coals. I have long forgotten the test score (or even who the opposition was), but I can still remember that almost-raw tuna with its whisper of flame-grilled flavour.

Obviously my memory for food is much stronger than my memory for sport. For example, the mere word "rugby" is enough to conjure up the braaivleis and beer of my youth. In rural France we drink red wine rather than beer and when a fire is lit outside it may be simply for flashing a piece of fish over coals so quickly that it almost tastes like sushi. But meat remains important for most of the men here who are rugby fans – and Theo is no exception. We're talking about "real" meat, red meat, beef, steak, oxtail and other such joys.

On our side of the Rhône, live cattle are never seen. It's a dry region of sheep and goats, vines and olives. Theo lives across the river in Nîmes, on the fringe of the Camargue, a marshy landscape known for black bulls as well as white horses. Nîmes is also one of a number of southern cities where Spanish traditions such as sangria, paella and bull fights are upheld with enthusiasm. Personally, I am not an advocate of bullfighting. You can quote Hemingway or Picasso at me until you are blue in the face, but I won't be convinced. I have nothing against a succulent, rare steak, but I don't want to see an animal tormented en route to my plate. I know, I know – it's

as irrational as saying "yes, please" to beef and lamb and "no thank you" to horse or pig. But the palate, like the heart, has its own reason.

When the Springboks won the World Cup in 2007, we gathered at Theo and Christine's house to watch the match. By that time Alain and I, not normally rugby watchers, were thoroughly infected by the fever that had raged for months in the host country. We watched every match in which South Africa or France was involved – at first out of a sense of duty until, somewhere along the way, duty turned to delight. I am still sorry that there was no clash between the Springboks and the French. I know whom I would have cheered for – but it would have been interesting to see where my children's loyalties lay.

On the joyful evening of the final, we dined royally, as always at Theo and Christine's. Among the guests were French-South African couples like Stephan and Elmarie, and in honour of the occasion we organised a few traditional South African dishes. My pumpkin fritters with cinnamon sugar were warmly received – including by some of the French – which delighted me because they are among the beloved treats of my childhood that my own children refuse to enjoy. Like *melkkos*, which can still reduce me to maudlin homesickness.

Of course we also ate meat: South African bobotie and a French bredie, because red meat and rugby belong together. Even if the meat is not grilled outside over an open fire, but braised very slowly indoors on a stove. A bredie, which the French call a *daube* or a *ragoût*, is a splendid way to cook meat with vegetables, "*so intimately stewed that the flesh is thoroughly impregnated with the vegetable flavour while the vegetables have benefited from the meat juices.*" Thus the great South African poet and food writer C Louis Leipoldt. And if you still need convincing, please go ahead and try Theo's recipe for a tomato-flavoured oxtail bredie.

Right: Tomato and oxtail bredie

TOMATO AND OXTAIL BREDIE

SERVES 6-8

A flavoursome combination of French and South African cooking methods, the meat can literally be left to cook for hours until tender. Do remember, however, to skim off the fat from time to time, warns Theo, because a bredie should never be greasy – once again, according to no less an authority than Leipoldt.

1,8 kg oxtail, cut into pieces | 3 large carrots, peeled | 3 large onions, peeled | 1-2 garlic cloves, finely chopped | 1,5 litres red wine | 1-2 bay leaves | 2-3 T olive oil | 2 kg tomatoes | 15 g fresh ginger, grated (or a pinch of powdered ginger) | 1-2 T chutney | fresh thyme, rosemary and coriander | a pinch of cardamom (seeds or powder) | salt and pepper

Begin the previous day with the marinade. Place the meat, carrots, onions and garlic in a dish. Add the wine, plus a few sprigs of thyme and rosemary and the bay leaves. Leave to stand for 24 hours in a cool place, turning the meat now and then so that it becomes thoroughly soaked in the marinade.

Remove the meat and vegetables, strain the marinade through a sieve, and reduce by boiling 1-2 cups of the strained liquid for 10 minutes.

Heat 2 T olive oil in a large heavy-based pot and brown the meat well. Plunge the tomatoes into boiling water, peel and cut into quarters. (You could also add green tomatoes.) Add to the pot with the meat. Slice the carrots and onions and add to the pot with the ginger, chopped coriander leaves and cardamom. Simmer over a low heat for a few hours.

Season with salt and pepper to taste. Add the chutney and a little of the reduced marinade – just a little because a bredie must be succulent, but definitely not watery.

Serve with steaming white rice or boiled potatoes.

CHOCOLATE, ONE MORE TIME …

"CHOCOLATE IS THE BEST FRIEND OF THOSE ENGAGED IN LITERARY PURSUITS."
BARON JUSTUS VON LIEBIG (1803-1873)

Years ago, at the legendary Hotel Negresco in Nice, I chatted to the chef of its equally famous restaurant …

And now that I've grabbed everyone's attention with that opening sentence, let me confess at once. I was there as a hardworking journalist, writing a food story for a magazine, and not as a regular guest.

At the time I was also a single mother, so I had to drag my little boy along with me. Daniel was more impressed with the "gold" taps in the bathroom than with the magnificent food on our plates. The only solution was a shameless bribe. "Be a very good boy while Mommy eats the Negresco's food and I'll take you to McDonald's afterwards." It worked like a charm. But towards the end of the meal, when the chef came to our table to talk, Daniel became more and more fidgety and finally let out a despairing wail: "Mommy, I'm hungry! When are we going to McDonald's?"

Before I could creep under the table with embarrassment, the king of that gastronomic palace admitted with a broad grin that he loved indulging in a Big Mac on a Sunday evening when he returned from a weekend of skiing. That was his *péché mignon*, his "cute little sin", which is what the French call these inexplicable cravings and secret addictions.

MFK Fisher once dedicated a whole sensual essay to "*secret eatings*". Her weakness was for tangerine segments, which she would bake for hours on the radiator in her lodgings and then leave for a few minutes in the snow on the windowsill. "*I cannot tell you why they are so magical. Perhaps it is that little shell, thin as one layer of enamel on a Chinese bowl, that crackles so tinily, so ultimately under your teeth. Or the rush of cold pulp just after it. Or the perfume. I cannot tell.*"

After I read this ode, of course I couldn't resist the temptation to try her way of eating tangerines. It is indeed an enchanting experience – but it didn't become my *péché mignon*. At school I had a friend who devoured beetroot with peanut butter. In secret, because she could not explain to the rest of us why she found it so irresistible. I know quite a few meat-eaters who enjoy nibbling raw sausage. Other respectable souls have a weakness for raw dough. My husband's pet vice is soup; nothing odd about that, but his timing always raises eyebrows. He's mad about it for breakfast.

My *péché mignon* is not nearly so original. It's probably the most common secret eating habit in the world. I'm talking about the chocolate that I hide in my bedroom to sweeten my dreams.

Because it's such a common sin – unlike beetroot with peanut butter – I don't always have to keep it secret. Chocolate is, thank heaven, a respectable way to end a meal – unlike tangerines toasted on a boarding house radiator. And however delicious a dessert of perfect fresh fruit may be, my tongue often feels like a child that won't go to sleep without a bedtime story.

Chocolate is my bedtime story. Not that I want the whole saga every time. Just as you can soothe a child with a little piece of a story before her eyes close, so my tongue finds comfort in a single handmade chocolate truffle with strong coffee at the end of a meal. Or perhaps two tiny squares, broken off the slab that I keep near my pillow.

Early Meso-American cultures believed that cocoa was a magical potion that would impart wisdom and power. Almost two centuries ago, the German chemist Baron Von Liebig described chocolate as a "*complete food*". And modern science has proved that chocolate with a high percentage of cocoa has properties that can indeed be described as magical. When you eat good chocolate, endorphins are released in your brain, inducing the same euphoric feeling as being in love.

That's why I steadfastly believe that chocolate provides a perfect ending for absolutely anything – whether it's a companionable meal, a difficult day, or a book of food stories.

CHOCOLATE MOUSSE WITH LEMON VERBENA
(OR MINT, OR RED FRUIT, OR ANYTHING ACTUALLY) ***
SERVES 4

Chocolate mousse has an inexplicable reputation as a "difficult" dessert to make at home. In fact it's one of the simplest sweets in the world to conjure up yourself. All you really need is good chocolate and the whites of a few eggs.

I have tested stacks of recipes, some with sugar, others with egg yolks, others with cream or a few drops of alcohol or spices or herbs … and the simplest of all, with only chocolate and egg whites, remains my favourite.

Of course you can decorate it with mint leaves or add lemon verbena or grate orange rind over it or crown it with berries if you feel so inspired. With this one very basic chocolate mousse you can create a new dessert every time – and be sure that every one will be a winner.

200 g dark chocolate (at least 50% cocoa, preferably more) | *4 egg whites* | *a pinch of salt* | *1 sprig lemon verbena (optional)* | *1 t sugar (optional)*

Melt the chocolate in a glass bowl over a pot of boiling water.

Whip the egg whites in a glass bowl with a pinch of salt until stiff. Stir half the egg whites quickly into the chocolate with a whisk, and fold in the other half carefully with a flat spoon. (I must confess that I have by accident done it the other way round – first folding and then beating – and the mousse still turned out fine.)

If you like, you can now add the lemon verbena. Chop it finely, mix it with the sugar and sprinkle over the mousse. Leave it in the fridge for at least an hour – and thank heaven once again for the wonder of chocolate.

MOUSSE OR CREAM? ***
Many people are not clear on the difference between a *mousse au chocolat* and a *crème au chocolat*. The latter has a smoother, creamier taste, as you would expect from the name. The *crèmes* that you buy in plastic cups sometimes taste of nothing but candyfloss, only good enough for children who don't know any better. A mousse has a richer more spongy flavour – almost as though you can taste the air bubbles incorporated with the egg whites – and a more "muddy" texture, such as good melted chocolate will provide. And what heavenly mud it is too.

Right: Chocolate mousse with lemon verbena

INDISPENSABLE

"BY ECONOMY AND GOOD MANAGEMENT, BY A SPARING USE OF
READY MONEY, AND BY PAYING SCARCELY ANYBODY, PEOPLE CAN
MANAGE, FOR A TIME AT LEAST, TO MAKE A GREAT SHOW
WITH VERY LITTLE MEANS."

WILLIAM MAKEPEACE THACKERAY (1811-1863)

This last chapter is about a few basic preparation methods, sauces, herbs and other information that is indispensable if you want "*to make a great show with very little means*". Nowadays *pistou*, mayonnaise, shortcrust pastry and other staples can all be bought, but they nearly always taste nicer and provide more satisfaction if you make them yourself.

CHOOSING CHERVIL

If you can't find chervil, you can substitute parsley or coriander. And if you don't know what chervil is you don't need to feel an ignoramus. It's very rarely found in Anglo-Saxon cookbooks, but the French cannot manage without it. They call it *cerfeuil* (*Anthriscus cerefolium*) and it's a herb that looks rather like parsley but with a milder flavour. In fact the taste is so subtle that it doesn't survive the cooking process and is therefore rather used in salads or snipped over hot dishes.

Even in France it's hard to find because it wilts so quickly. Essentially, it's a garden herb – or, as with us, one that grows effortlessly in a pot on the kitchen windowsill, always in easy reach.

BOUQUET GARNI

Bouquet garni means literally a "trimmed bunch" of fresh herbs, traditionally bound with the leaf of a leek. Today a piece of string is the usual tie but the herbs may also be placed in a small porous bag like a tea bag. There is no generic recipe for the herbs, but thyme, bay leaves and parsley are almost always included and often rosemary, sage or basil as well.

BEST, AVAILABLE, AFFORDABLE

Contrary to current fashion, I have decided not to describe each seasoning or ingredient for every recipe in detail. I feel it's needlessly prescriptive to emphasise time and again that I prefer to use grey salt from Guerande (the best salt that you can buy in France and perhaps in the world), or freshly ground black pepper, or extra virgin olive oil from the first cold pressing of the olives.

I assume rather that all enthusiastic cooks will use the best available and affordable ingredients – and I know from experience that the words "available" and "affordable" are as important as "best". Sometimes you simply cannot afford the best, or you do not have it to hand and then you cook with what you have.

The most important ingredients of all in any dish are the love and enjoyment with which you set about its preparation.

PESTO OR *PISTOU*

For Provençal *pistou*, crush 3-4 peeled garlic cloves with 20-30 large basil leaves and a pinch of salt. You can pound it in the old-fashioned way in a mortar if you're in an authentic mood – or you can use a food processor. Add 125 g Parmesan cheese, and then 125 ml olive oil in a thin stream, stirring all the time (or use an electric beater) until you get a thick green paste. For Italian pesto you add a quarter of a cup of roasted pine nuts to the first three ingredients.

CLASSIC FRENCH VINAIGRETTE

The easiest way to make about 150 ml vinaigrette is to put 2 tablespoons white or red wine vinegar, 6 tablespoons olive oil, 1-2 teaspoons Dijon mustard and a pinch of sugar in a glass jar, screw the lid on tight and shake well. Season with salt and pepper to taste. You can also add 1-2 crushed garlic cloves and fresh herbs of your choice, finely chopped.

SHORTCRUST PASTRY

For about 250 g pastry, you need 250 g flour, 75 g butter cut into pieces, 1 egg and a pinch of salt. Sift the flour into a mixing bowl and rub in the butter with your fingers until the mixture looks like fine breadcrumbs. Add the egg, salt and a few tablespoons of water to make a soft dough. (If you want to use the dough for a sweet tart or dessert, add 50 g sugar and a little more water.) Cover the dough with clingfilm and allow to rest in the fridge for at least 30 minutes before using. You can also make larger quantities and keep it in the fridge for 2-3 days to use as you need.

MAYONNAISE

For about 150 ml mayonnaise, use 1 egg yolk, 150 ml olive oil, 3-4 teaspoons white wine vinegar (or lemon juice) and a pinch of salt. It's important that the ingredients and your utensils should be at room temperature. Whisk the egg yolk in a bowl. Add the olive oil drop by drop, whisking continuously. When the mayonnaise begins to thicken, continue adding the olive oil, but in a thin, constant stream. Keep whisking until all the oil is absorbed. Season with salt and add the vinegar or lemon juice.

COULIS DE TOMATE

For about 700 ml *coulis* you need 1 kg tomatoes, 1 large onion and a pinch of salt. Slice the tomatoes, place in a saucepan with their juice and pulp, and sprinkle with salt. You can also add a finely chopped garlic clove and herbs such as basil, parsley and thyme, also finely chopped. Simmer for 10 minutes over a low heat without adding any water. (If the tomatoes are not juicy enough, you can add not more than half a cup of water.) Raise the heat a little and cook the tomatoes for another 20 minutes over a medium heat, stirring now and then. Remove from the stove and allow to cool.

Blitz in a food processor and strain the thick juice through a sieve to remove the skins. Pour into a jar and store in the fridge. Use with rice or meatballs or pasta, or of course with the famous *pain d'aubergine* (eggplant loaf). It will instantly become an indispensable ingredient in your kitchen.

AUBERGINE – TO SALT OR NOT TO SALT?

Recipes that include aubergines often recommend that you salt the slices and leave them in a colander for half an hour to draw out the bitterness, as the old people would say. We usually don't bother, because modern aubergines are bred and grown to taste less bitter. But it can be useful because a salted aubergine doesn't absorb as much oil when it's fried. In the case of a tian, the salting process can also help to dry out the aubergine a little, which is important because a tian, unlike ratatouille, should not be bathed in sauce.

As so often with cooking, there is no hard and fast rule. It depends on the dish you're making, the quality of the aubergine you're using, on how bitter or oily or dry you like your food – and sometimes simply on how soon you want to eat.

ACKNOWLEDGEMENTS

If writing may be compared to dining, then my previous books were modest meals for one. To write fiction I have to have solitude, isolation and silence; that's the only way I can do it. This book, however, was another story altogether – a banquet that a whole throng of workers helped me prepare.

Now, like my Gallic friends, who only pour the champagne with the dessert – and propose the toasts at the end of the meal – I would like to raise my glass to thank everyone.

Without my husband, Alain, there would have been no book – and often no food on the table either while I was busy writing these food stories. As I have explained on page 103, it all began with his onion soup and it was his patience and enthusiasm that kept the whole project on the boil. For months he tested recipes over and over until we arrived at the final versions for the book. While Lien Botha was in Provence doing the photography, he would rise at the crack of dawn and work with us late into the evening. He was always a willing chauffeur and cook and also played his part in the photo sessions (somewhat less willingly, but always with good humour). *Merci, mon amour.*

Merci also to our children, Thomas, Hugo, Daniel and Mia, who had to taste all the food in the book and were always ready with their opinions. Thomas and Hugo were not able to take part in last summer's photo sessions because they had holiday jobs elsewhere, so Daniel and Mia had more than their fair share of work to do. Tree climbing, going to market, riding bicycles, walking, talking and above all, eating, all sound like fun but can soon become tedious when you have to keep doing them in front of a camera.

That's why I'm endlessly grateful for a photographer like Lien, who has the amazing gift of invisibility. Time after time our family and guests forgot completely that we were being photographed. In fact sometimes we enjoyed ourselves so much that we even forgot to leave a bite of food for the poor hardworking photographer ...

Many thanks to friends who supplied recipes and helped with photo sessions: Renée Greyling and Annika and Serge Remusan of Domaine Chapoton in Rochegude; Theo and Christine Meyer and their children, and Stephan and Elmarie Landwerlin, all of Nîmes; Gavin, Glenda and Michaela Younge of Cape Town, who also made their holiday home available to the photographer. Peta Wolpe also provided accommodation for Lien – appropriately in the same cottage where my own Provençal adventure began in 1996.

Other friends, and friends of our children, were sometimes persuaded – with a plate of food, what else – to model for Lien or to help with photos at short notice: Hakima Mriouah, Anita Katouache, Théo Bonin-Voirol, Stanley Rayne, Tess Voncopenole, Marie-Laure Davezan and her children; Mario, Yvette and Maxime Maruccia of Réunion and Canada; the Goedegebeure-Van Niekerk-Avis family of Holland and the Hoogenbooms of New York.

Just like a real Hollywood production there was, in addition to the French crew, an extremely able Cape Town team involved in the project. My thanks to the commissioning editor, Ansie Kamffer, who always knew precisely what she wanted and was able to inspire the creative team, in particular the translator Laurian Brown, editor Vanessa Vineall, designer Anton Sassenberg, food photographer Jan Ras, stylist Sonja Jordt, food-assistant Johané van Schalkwyk, picture researcher Anna Erasmus, indexer Anna Tanneberger, typesetter Wim Reinders, production manager Ilse Volschenk, editorial assistant Lindy Samery, Ben Page, Maria Cronjé, Carine Le Roux, publicist Surita Joubert and the NB Publishers sales team.

I raise a glass to all of you. Virginia Woolf said: *"One cannot think well, love well, sleep well, if one has not dined well."* Let us try always to eat better, so that we can sleep, think and love better. Cheers! Or as we say in France: *Santé!*

BIBLIOGRAPHY

Besides the background information and the quotations on food that I sourced on the internet; and besides the recipes that have been used in our kitchen for so long and amended so often that we have no idea where they came from originally; and besides the lessons which I have learnt down the years about food and about writing from Afrikaans food writers such as Nettie Pikeur, Mariëtte Crafford, Marlene van Niekerk and Braam Kruger (gone but unforgettable), there were also a number of books that I turned to regularly while working on *Summer Food in Provence*.

1001 Foods You Must Try Before You Die; edited by Frances Case; Quintessence, London, 2008.

A Guide to Modern Cookery; Auguste Escoffier; first edition, 1909; Bracken Books, London, 1994.

An Omelette and a Glass of Wine; Elizabeth David; Penguin, London, 1986. (Although this is the only one of David's books from which I quote directly, her first five books can all be regarded as inspiring sources for *Summer Food in Provence*: *Mediterranean Food*, 1950; *French Country Cooking*, 1951; *Italian Food*, 1954; *Summer Cooking*, 1955; *French Provincial Cooking*, 1960 – all published by Penguin.)

Bon Comme Là-Bas!; Editions Solar, France, 2006.

Culinaria – European Specialties; edited by Joachim Römer and Michael Ditter; first edition, 1995; Könemann, Cologne, 2000.

La Cuisine Provençale du Mas Tourteron; Elisabeth Bourgeois; Editions du Chêne, Paris, 1996.

One Hundred Years of Solitude; Gabriel García Márquez; first edition in Spanish, Argentina, 1967; Picador, London, 1978. (Not really a food book, but still my favourite hammock reading when I'm worn out with cooking or writing.)

The Art of Eating; MFK Fisher; first edition, 1954; Macmillan, New York, 1990. (An omnibus of five of Fisher's highly entertaining books that were published in the nineteen thirties and forties: *Serve It Forth*; *Consider the Oyster*; *How to Cook a Wolf*; *The Gastronomical Me*; *An Alphabet for Gourmets*.)

INDEX